AIRACOBRA ADVANTAGE: The Flying Cannon

The Complete Story of Bell Aircraft Corporation's P-39 Pursuit Fighter Plane

AIRACOBRA ADVANTAGE: The Flying Cannon

The Complete Story of Bell Aircraft Corporation's P-39 Pursuit Fighter Plane

by Rick Mitchell

PICTORIAL HISTORIES PUBLISHING COMPANY
Missoula, Montana

LIBRARY OF CONGRESS
CATALOG CARD NO. 92-80004

ISBN 0-929521-62-5

First Printing: March 1992

Typography: Arrow Graphics
Cover Layout: Mike Egeler

COVER PHOTO: The world's only two presently flying P-39s, currently owned by the Kalamazoo Aviation History Museum (left) and the Confederate Air Force (right). COURTESY KALAMAZOO AVIATION HISTORY MUSEUM

BACK COVER: A P-39 magazine advertisement from early World War Two. COURTESY BELL AIRCRAFT CORPORATION

PICTORIAL HISTORIES PUBLISHING COMPANY
713 South Third West
Missoula, Montana 59801

FOREWORD

The United States Army Air Force operated five different fighter planes worldwide during the Second World War. Two were pursuit fighters available when the war began that continued in the action until the conflict was over, the P-39 and the P-40. The other three, the P-38, P-47 and the P-51, were introduced during the war and finished the task the first two started. Each fighter accomplished its mission exceptionally well.

"The P-39 was truly a fine airplane when utilized for the mission for which it was designed. Many articles written by misinformed authors and/or unqualified pilots have adversely affected the reputation of a fine airplane," stated A. M. "Tex" Johnston, former Chief Test Pilot with Bell Aircraft Corporation and Thompson Trophy winner in 1946 with *Cobra II*, in a letter to the author dated April 16, 1990.

This is the history of Bell Aircraft Corporation's P-39 Airacobra. It includes each variant and spinoff version, comparisons with other contemporary fighter aircraft, personal accounts of testing and flying the P-39, histories of all known surviving Airacobras in the world today, and an assortment of photographs. This is a detailed account of the Airacobra from a 1990s vantage point, almost fifty years after the last P-39 was assembled.

DEDICATION

This book is dedicated to Larry Bell and the thousands of men and women who designed, assembled, tested, repaired and flew the P-39 and the P-400 Airacobras. These were the people who poured their lives into the successful development and deployment of this fighter plane. May their dedication never be taken for granted nor forgotten.

A special dedication and remembrance is further made to those pilots both at Bell Aircraft Corporation and with the Armed Forces who made the ultimate sacrifice for their country while testing and flying the Airacobra:

IN MEMORY OF THOSE AIRACOBRA PILOTS
WHO DIED IN THE LINE OF DUTY.

MAY THEY NEVER BE FORGOTTEN.

CONTENTS

THE STORY BEHIND THE BOOK

Airacobra Advantage is intended to be a well researched history of available data and recollections of surviving individuals about the complete history of the Bell P-39 and P-400 Airacobras. It is the result of many hours of research, reviewing internal Bell Aircraft Corporation publications and other published material, telephone calls and letters throughout the United States and several foreign countries, and data comparison. Finally, interviews were conducted with several highly respected individuals who were acquainted with the Airacobra. Many dedicated people have allowed the author the benefit of their expertise. Special thanks are given to the following individuals who generously offered their assistance in many ways toward the completion of this book: David W. Allen*, Ralph M. Bartholomew, Col. Paul S. Bechtel, Dave Bennett, Henry A. Brown, Joseph Cannon, John T. Correll, Barbara Cushner, Robert E. Ellis, Louis Eltscher, Col. Charles Falletta, John P. Haynes, Col. Kenneth Heller, Lola Hilton, Stan Hoefler, Frederick A. Johnsen, A. M. "Tex" Johnston,* Frank "Chick" Lajudice, Gary Larkins, Robert Leder, Col. Robert P. Lowe, Jr., Ed Maloney, Edmund S. Marek, Ivan G. M'bagintao, Dorothy E. Mitchell, Col. Jesse D. Mitchell, Jr.,* Bob Ogden, Michael O'Leary, Dennis Parks, Betty Haas Pfister, Paul Poberezny, Jack B. Prior, Edward J. Roseler, Al Salandra, Col. Virgil E. "Sandy" Sansing, Andrea Shaw, Geraldine D. Schluderberg, Lt. Col. William A. Shomo, Blake W. Smith, Ted Spencer, Vincent W. Steffanic, James W. Swinnitch, Col. Bruce F. Tuxill,* Hannu Valtonen, Nick Veronico, Nick Watling, Don Whittington, Larry Wilson, Brigadier General Chuck Yeager.

*Denotes review committee members who reviewed the prototype text.

Additional thanks are expressed to Mr. Truman A. Partridge, Sr., a former Bell Aircraft Corporation illustrator with a keen interest in the P-39. He loaned the author many photographs seen in this book as well as copies of research data he developed years ago on the P-39. His help is greatly appreciated.

Last, but certainly not least, my sincerest thanks to Dr. William Windover.* When I decided to write this book, several calls led to the Amherst Colony Museum, where some of Bell's early records are stored. They asked Dr. Windover to contact me. Dr. Windover works for the New York State Senate. He has an avid and generous interest in the P-39. With his help, many individuals and information areas were made available that otherwise would not have been accessible. The result was a better narrative. I was extremely fortunate to have Dr. Windover's invaluable assistance.

I was born into a fighter pilot's family, although I am not a pilot myself. My father was a World War Two P-40 and P-51 pilot who later joined the Air National Guard. Over the years, I read everything I found interesting on aviation, especially stories about World War Two fighter planes. In 1989, after writing newsletters and magazine articles for many years, I wrote the *History of the Maryland Air National Guard*. When that book was completed, I began building radio-controlled model airplanes again. I wanted to build a World War Two fighter plane for a change, but one with good ground handling and classic fighter lines. The only viable choice was a P-39 Airacobra. While finishing this balsa model, it amazed me that little documentation material was available. By January 1990, I located a P-39Q nearby at the Paul E. Garber restoration facility in Silver Hill, Maryland, the site where the planes for the National Air and Space Museum are restored. I photographed their Airacobra, *Galloping Gertie*, which was in an excellent unrestored condition. I soon decided to write the history of the Bell P-39 Airacobra, as there had never been one complete text written before. I felt the Airacobra deserved better recognition than it had received over the last 45 years. Another aspect that was truly annoying was that too much that was written was unreasonably negative about the P-39. This book shows the P-39 for what it was, one of America's true military aerial strengths during the first years of World War Two. My hope is that some day there will be more restored Airacobras at our air shows or in our museums, and that visitors will look proudly when they see one and say, "That was an excellent airplane and a true contributor to the war effort." I personally hope the good folks at the National Air and Space Museum will soon take *Galloping Gertie* from her public display storage area, put her through their excellent restoration shops, and display her downtown at the major museum. She deserves to be displayed in the same grand halls as her cousins, a beautifully detailed P-51 and a P-40. If more restored P-39s are placed before the viewing public in the years to come, then I will look back proudly some day and say I accomplished the job I set out to do.

Rick Mitchell
Airacobra Advantage
1991

INTRODUCTION

"The Legend of the Flying Cobras"

Consider this question about World War Two for a moment: "Would aviation history remember the P-39 more favorably today if General Chennault had been supplied with Airacobras on the eve of World War Two instead of P-40 Warhawks for his Flying Tigers?" Consider the following three *fictionalized* paragraphs of history, which are an adaptation of parts of pages 489 to 492 of *The Army Air Forces In World War Two, Volume One,* written by Wesley Craven and James Cate, published in 1948 for the Office of Air Force History:

> "A cardinal feature of General Chennault's plan in China during late 1941 was to avoid committing his force until it had been thoroughly trained. But after 7 December 1941 and the Japanese attack on Pearl Harbor, Rangoon, chief port of entry for supplies reaching China, came under threat of Japanese attack. One squadron of the AVG, the American Volunteer Group, was sent to Mingaladon on 12 December. During the following week, the other two squadrons were moved east to Kunming for protection of the Burma Road. There, the AVG pilots first entered combat, when on 20 December, they inflicted heavy loss on Japanese bombers attempting attack on Kunming while using the overwhelming firepower of their forward fuselage 37mm cannons against the enemy. Three days later, the P-39Ds at Mingaladon inflicted comparable damage on a formation of enemy planes attacking Rangoon.
>
> "The Airacobras in their operations followed closely preconceived tactical patterns. Using two-ship elements in hit-and-run tactics, the pilots extracted the fullest advantage from the superior diving, heavy firepower and low-level speed of the P-39, while nullifying the enemy fighters' superiority in maneuverability and rate of climb by avoiding dogfights. Against the bombers they also used a diving attack, frequently coming out of the dive to strike the bombers from below. These tactics enabled Chennault's 'Flying Cobras' to destroy an almost incredible number of the more fragile Japanese planes while sustaining minimum losses.
>
> "By early 1942, pilots of the 23rd Fighter Group began to arrive as replacements for the AVG."

Possibly the answer to our question is yes. Had the "Flying Tigers" been the "Flying Cobras" with P-39s instead of P-40s, the Airacobras might be more favorably remembered today. The Flying Tigers are remembered as America's first successful flying group during the Second World War, raising the P-40 in esteem with a saddened American nation during the darkest days of the early war, but the P-39D could certainly have performed the role described above for the P-40 in true history.

Try this experiment the next time you are speaking with a group of friendly aviation experts: Ask them what they think about the P-40. The answer will most likely be that it was an excellent airplane, and in truth it surely was. Then ask what the consensus of opinion is about the Bell P-39 Airacobra? Unfortunately you may be told it was a poor performer, or that it left much to be desired. But the facts do not bear these last responses out. The truth is that no model of the P-40 during its entire service history was ever as fast as the slowest P-39 variant. No P-40 was ever armed with the tremendous firepower or knockout punch carried by every P-39. Why does the P-39 carry such a tarnished image among aviation historians almost fifty years later? Because too many aviation enthusiasts continue making the mistake of comparing the P-39, America's earliest modern fighter plane, with much later World War Two fighter designs America produced, such as the P-38, the P-47, and the supreme World War Two fighter of all time powered by a piston engine, the P-51. But these were fighter planes designed for a *different* mission than the P-39, and they were developed *much later* in the war, when fighter requirements had changed. In the years before and during early World War Two, the P-39 was America's most advanced pursuit aircraft. It was, however, a non-turbo-supercharged pursuit fighter, developed this way at the Army Air Corps' request, and designed for coastal defense and ground support, a mission it *excelled* at during the entire war. It was *never* designed to be a high-altitude, long-range escort fighter such as the P-51 was.

Our purpose is to not let old myths deceive aviation enthusiasts any longer about the P-39 and to tell the true story behind the Airacobra. It was one of America's most successful World War Two fighters, performing the mission assigned to it *better* than any other American fighter in World War Two. Judge for yourself where its place in aviation history rightfully *should be.*

The Bell P-39 Airacobra was one of the most heroic pursuit/fighter aircraft developed and flown before and during World War Two. Here, then, is its complete story . . .

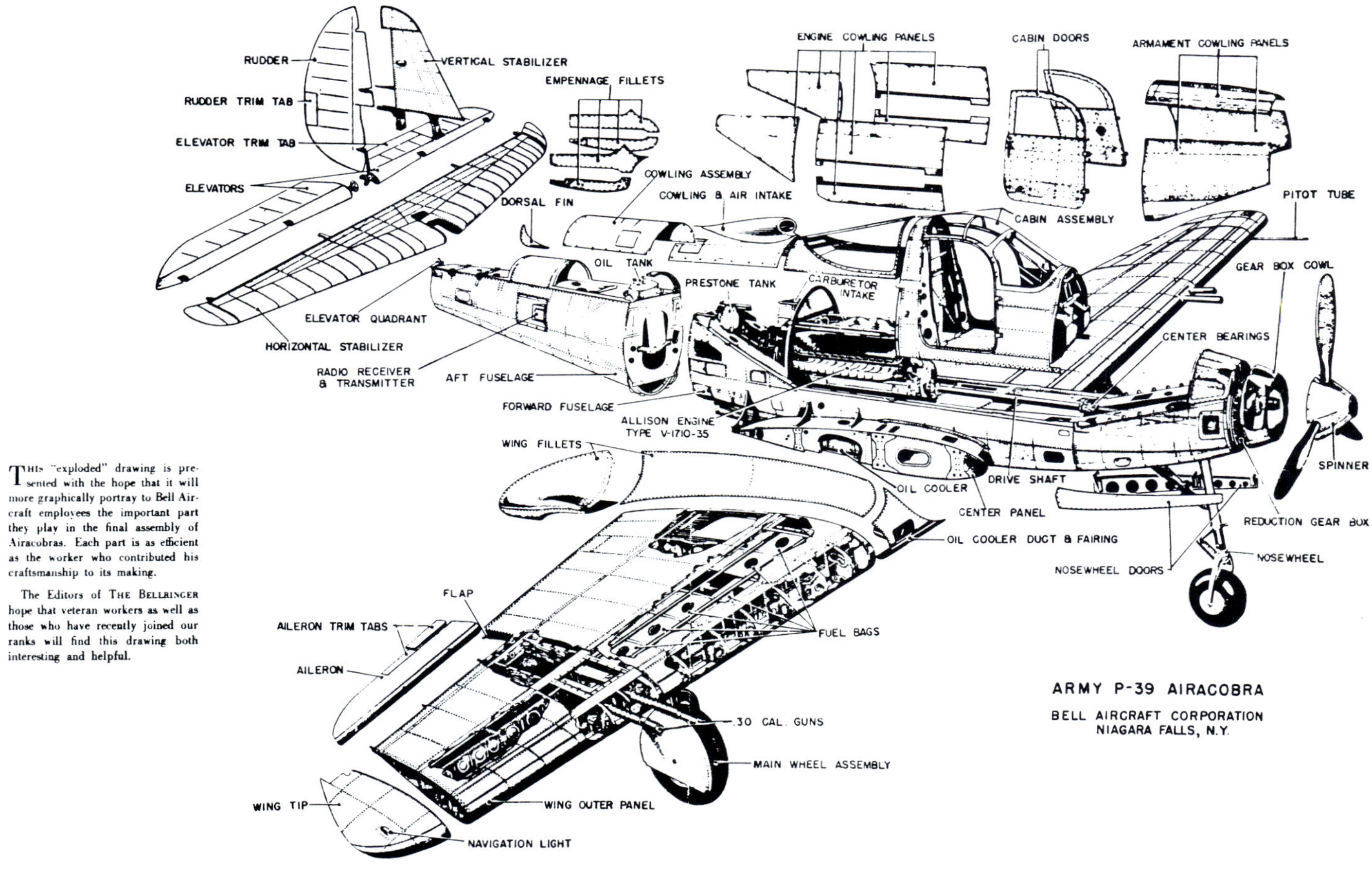

Exploded view of a P-39 from a Bell magazine, *The Bellringer.* BELL AIRCRAFT CORP. VIA EDMUND S. MAREK

WE Beat THE AXIS TO IT...

America has been "on the alert." In spite of long years of building an evil war machine, the Axis will find that American science and industry are still far ahead. More than five years ago Bell Aircraft initiated ideas in aircraft design which allow the Bell Airacobra to carry the world's heaviest fire power among single engine fighters. In helping to give America mastery in the sky, it's a reassuring fact that the Airacobra began to get the benefits of Bell Aircraft's technical and experimental resources five years before it was to be called on to prove its practical superiority.

BELL Aircraft CORPORATION

BUFFALO, NEW YORK, U. S. A.

Making Aviation History

THE HISTORY OF THE AIRACOBRA

The decade of the Thirties was a period of unsettled change on many political and military fronts. War clouds were forming over several European and Pacific nations. What was once peace for many countries was slowly slipping away, and an uncertain future lay ahead.

To combat these changes, or perhaps to provoke them, many industrialized nations were advancing the state of their military art. This evolution was perhaps most noticeable in the field of military aviation. A new generation of aerial bombers and fighters was being developed in Germany and Japan at an alarmingly fast pace, and the United States was badly behind. America was theoretically losing the war long before the first shots were fired.

By the mid-1930s, the United States was flying many graceful yet outdated pursuit aircraft (the term "pursuit" being correct long before "fighter" became accepted in May 1942). By the end of the decade, America's Republic P-35s and Curtiss P-36s were woefully inadequate for combat use. Both were low-wing single-seat pursuit aircraft possessing maximum speeds of only 310 miles per hour. To counter the threat of the German Bf-109s and Japanese Zeros, America's newer Bell P-39s and Curtiss P-40s were introduced. They were advanced aircraft, but as aviation history has shown, they were interim fighters, though both performed well against overwhelming odds on many major war fronts. They were the most modern pursuit aircraft designed and built in the United States during the dismal days of early World War Two. The P-39 and the P-40 made up more than half of the Army Air Force's inventory of fighter planes until January 1943, with more than half of those in overseas combat until September 1943. Both fought long and hard until more advanced fighter aircraft such as the P-38, P-47 and P-51 became available years later. Without the P-39 and the P-40, the Second World War may have had a prolonged or different outcome.

This is the story of the P-39, Bell's contribution to America's war effort.

The History of Bell Aircraft Corporation

On July 10, 1935, a new aircraft company was incorporated in Buffalo, New York. Its founder and president was Lawrence Dale Bell who was formerly with Consolidated Aircraft Company. Larry Bell was age 41. He had been a mechanic with the Glenn L. Martin Company, another large aircraft manufacturer, and eventually became a general manager. He later went with Consolidated where he became a Vice President. In 1935, Consolidated moved its company west from Buffalo to San Diego, California. Bell resigned and formed his own company. He hired many former Consolidated workers in Buffalo to work for his fledgling company, the Bell Aircraft Corporation.

Bell Aircraft designed a long line of innovative and well made aircraft. Among them were the Bell P-59 Airacomet, America's first jet-powered fighter plane, and the Bell X-1 and X-2 series, the rocket-powered sound barrier breaking planes from the late '40s and '50s. Bell Aerospace/Textron and Bell Helicopter/Textron today are two of the largest military hardware and helicopter manufacturers in the world.

Bell's chief design engineer in the 1930s was Robert J. Woods. He was 31 when Bell Aircraft Corporation was formed. He already had an impressive list of advanced aviation designs to his credit despite having received a degree in aeronautical engineering only seven years earlier. He had worked with the Towle Aircraft Company, the Macraft Aircraft Company (as a consultant), the Detroit Aircraft Company, Lockheed and then Consolidated before joining Bell. He contributed to the designs of amphibian aircraft, torpedo bombers, and several earlier pursuit and attack aircraft for the Army, along with transport and record-setting speed aircraft. Along with his assistant, Harland Poyer, Mr. Woods' first project at Bell was the XFM-1 Airacuda, a twin Allison engine pusher fighter design. The Airacuda was the first all-Bell designed and built aircraft produced by Bell Aircraft Corporation. Bell had earlier assembled wing panels for Consolidated Aircraft Company and built one attack version of the PB-2Y flying boat, the A-11A. The A-11A used the new Allison V-1710 twelve cylinder (meaning pistons) inline engine, which later powered Bell's XFM-1 and the P-39. The Airacuda's two propellers were located behind the wing's trailing edge, effectively pushing the aircraft through the air. Allison aircraft engines were chosen because they were America's only inline engine that developed sufficient horsepower for the more modern aircraft designs. An inline engine is one whose pistons, cylinders and exhaust ports are placed in a straight line. This adds to the streamlining of the aircraft. An inline is different from a radial engine in that a radial has its pistons outlined in a circle and is much less aerodynamic. The P-35 and P-36 were powered by radial engines. They were less

Larry Bell displays one of his P-39s. Photo taken late 1941 or early 1942. An Airacobra I can be seen in the background. Mr. Bell's employee badge is seen on his lapel. BELL AIRCRAFT CORP. VIA TRUMAN A. PARTRIDGE, SR.

streamlined than the P-39 or the P-40, which both used inline engines. The term XFM-1 stood for "experimental fighter, multi-place." The XFM-1 was intended to be a "heavily-armed superfighter capable of destroying bombers." Bell's Airacuda underbid a similar design submitted by Lockheed Aircraft Corporation. Both aircraft had twin Allisons, but Bell's design was decisively more heavily gunned. The XFM-1 had many "firsts" to its credit. These included a modern tricycle landing gear, extension driveshafts for its engines, usage of Allison engines in a plane designed for that specific engine, and airborne 37mm cannons. These advanced concepts were put to good use later in Bell's second fighter design, the P-39. The XFM-1, however, was too costly at nearly double the price of a new Boeing B-17 four-engine bomber. An additional 13 YFM-1 prototype Airacudas were ordered, but these were the last of their breed. By January 1942, all FM-1s were flown to Chanute Field, Illinois. None ever saw combat.

Bell Plans Its Second Fighter Plane Design

With the P-35 and the P-36 approaching obsolescence, the Army Air Corps asked America's military aircraft manufacturers to develop new pursuit aircraft proposals. The Army called for a close support pursuit capable of coastal defense. The new aircraft were to defend our country's shores against invading foreign powers. It must be remembered that during the Thirties, many military planners believed the two major oceans on opposite sides of our country were our best defense. As long as these new pursuits defended our shores against the invader, they were accomplishing their mission. (The idea of a high-altitude interceptor fighter or long-range bomber escort fighter was not conceived until the United States was firmly entrenched in World War Two several years later).

Before and during the Second World War, many automobile manufacturers assembled war supplies. Buick, for example, built radial aircraft engines whereas Ford assembled B-24 four-engine bombers. In 1935, Oldsmobile developed a new 37mm cannon, the T-9, which was a weapon that fired larger individual explosive shells but at a slower rate than a rapid firing machine gun. The new cannon fired a 37 millimeter shell whose diameter was about one and a half inches, as compared to a .50 calibre machine gun bullet, which

Bell's chief design engineer and the Airacobra's designer, Robert J. Woods. The parachute doesn't fit his business suit! Photo taken around 1941. BELL AIRCRAFT CORP. VIA TRUMAN A. PARTRIDGE, SR.

The Model 3 proposal was developed in June 1936. The pilot sat behind the wing, which caused poor forward visibility. This photo was taken in May 1937, a week after the Model 4 had been submitted to the Army Air Corps. The Model 3 had generally been discarded by this time. See also pages 114 and 115 for several original factory sketches of the Model 4 proposal. BELL AIRCRAFT CORP. VIA EDMUND S. MAREK

is one-half inch in diameter. Design members from Bell watched the T-9's firing trials in May 1935 presented by the American Armament Corporation. When Bell designed its next aircraft after the Airacuda, they decided to build a pursuit aircraft around this deadly new weapon. The new Bell airplane introduced a new concept: a new weapons *system* (the P-39) designed to deliver a new *weapon* (the 37mm cannon) to its intended target.

In June 1936, Robert Woods and Harland Poyer developed two design proposals to fly the new cannon, the Bell Model 3 and Model 4. Because of the tremendous weight of the Oldsmobile cannon, the only logical place to mount the cannon was on the centerline, or middle of the wing and fuselage, and in the nose. To balance the weight of the cannon against the weight of the engine and the pilot, the Model 3 placed the engine in the center of the fuselage with the pilot behind, near the tail section; the Model 4, however, placed the pilot in the middle over the wing, and the engine behind the pilot. Both proposals featured a normal tractor or "pulling" propeller configuration with an Allison engine built into the fuselage. Both had nearly identical wing, landing gear and tail section dimensions and layouts. The dimensions and configurations, however, differed considerably in the fuselages. In time the Model 3 was discarded because of poor forward pilot visibility considerations caused by the pilot sitting so far back.

The Bell Model 4 was developed as a fast, altitude-climbing pursuit aircraft. Bell wanted it powered by a turbo-supercharged Allison engine. By using a turbo-supercharger, air coming into the engine was forced into the carburetor by means of a turbine spun by the engine's exhaust gases. This increased the performance of the engine at high altitudes, making the engine perform better, much like it did at lower altitudes. The Model 4 was the first design in the history of fighter aircraft in the United States where the pilot sat ahead of the engine, a concept that took a few pilots some getting used to. Today, almost all engines in fighter planes, although jet engines, are behind the pilot. The Model 4 transmitted its tremendous engine power through a ten foot extension driveshaft to a geared assembly or gearbox located behind the propeller. With this design, the section of the fuselage ahead of the pilot was freed to mount the new 37mm cannon, which fired its shells through the opened center hub of the propeller spinner.

Bell personnel performed extensive static design engineering testing to make the extension shaft design as problem-free as possible. Bell's engineers worked with personnel at Allison engines to accomplish this. Their analysis considered all forms of static and dynamic loads and their effect on the extension shaft as it was affected by the engine, propeller and the airframe itself during typical high-G combat maneuvers wherein the effect of gravity (G) was increased many times. The solution was to design a highly rigid forward fuselage to support the gear reduction assembly and the engine in one unit, supported by built-up beams with transverse framing made of aluminum. This gave an incredibly strong structure to support the engine in the rear and the propeller up front connected by the ten foot shaft. The assembly could withstand loads up to 12Gs, or twelve times the effect of the pull of gravity. Because there was additional room up front, Bell decided the new airplane would benefit from retractable tricycle or three strut landing gears, wherein a nose strut with a non-steerable but self-castering forward wheel would be located but hidden when retracted within the forward fuselage while in flight. Two main landing gears and wheels with shortened legs were then built into the wing behind the center of gravity, the balancing point of the plane from front to rear. The Model 4 featured two automobile-styled doors with roll-up windows for entry into both sides of the cockpit. The Model 4 proposal had a 35′ wingspan or length of the wing with a fuselage or main body length of 28′7½″. It proposed using a 10′ diameter propeller, and the main landing gears in the wing stood 10′6½″ apart. The length of the horizontal tail surfaces was 9′8″. The original Model 4's most noticeable outward difference was that the propeller attached to the rounded nose section of the fuselage and had no spinner cover to streamline it. Outwardly the Model 4 did resemble later production P-39s. A full-size mockup of the Model 4 proposal was completed as part of the design proposal in 1937.

Bell felt its new design offered improved maneuverability over any previous aircraft because the engine's weight was so close to the aircraft's center of gravity. Their design featured good external pilot visibility in all directions. The tricycle landing gear offered better ground handling and taxiing plus improved pilot vision while still on the ground. Finally, the open forward fuselage could accommodate heavy nose armament firing more accurately on the aircraft's centerline. The Bell Model 4 became the first truly modern low wing fighter plane designed in the United States prior to our entry into World War Two.

The New Pursuit Becomes Reality

In 1937, the Army Air Corps consisted of only three Pursuit Groups in the United States. The 1st Pursuit Group was based at Selfridge Field, Michigan; the 8th Pursuit Group was at Langley Field, Virginia; and the 20th Pursuit Group was located at Barksdale, Louisiana. The 8th Pursuit Group was equipped with Curtiss P-6E pursuit biplanes, a two-winged, fixed gear, obsolete fighter biplane. The 8th had three pursuit squadrons, the 33rd, 35th and 36th. The 8th Pursuit Group would later play a critical role in the defense of New Guinea and Australia in early World War Two flying P-39s.

In February 1937, the Army Air Corps called for a new experimental pursuit fighter plane having "the tactical mission of interception and attack of hostile aircraft at high altitude." The Army required a minimum airspeed of 360 miles per hour at altitude. The new pursuit would reach 20,000 feet in less than six minutes. The only engine that could deliver this performance was the Allison V-1710, which by February 1937 had not been tested at 1,000 horsepower. There were two ways to meet the Army's requirement: One was to design a new, fully streamlined aircraft to use the Allison efficiently. The other was to combine two Allison engines and design a new, twin-engine pursuit fighter. Bell and Curtiss used the former method with their P-39 and P-40, but Lockheed developed its twin-boom P-38 Lightning, a radical departure from current aircraft design thinking. Bell, however, placed the engine behind the pilot and developed a new pursuit with less frontal air resistance. Their Model 4 was also considerably lighter than contemporary pursuits with their engines in the forward fuselage.

On March 19, 1937, the Army Air Corps requested bids for the new pursuit. This was Type Specification Number X-609, calling for a one-pilot, one-engine pursuit fighter aircraft. It was later known as Project M-13-36. On May 18, 1937, Bell Aircraft submitted its Model 4 proposal to the Army for consideration. On October 7, 1937, the Army ordered one prototype of the Model 4 under contract number AC10341. The Army Air Corps also gave the Bell design its military designation, the XP-39. Earlier on June 23, the Army issued another contract, number AC9974, to Lockheed to build their prototype XP-38, which was given the Army Air Corps serial number 37-457. The prototype XP-38 Lightning flew on January 1, 1939, about three months before the Airacobra flew.

The design of the prototype XP-39 was not exactly the same as the proposal made to the Army in May 1937. The XP-39 went through considerable design changes before the prototype was completed in 1938. Additional scale model wind tunnel testing had been done, the Army Air Corps had ordered changes in the XP-39 as well as the development of the Allison engine, and the usual engineering revisions and changes in the design had occurred at Bell. The most noticeable outward design change was the addition of a propeller spinner streamlining the propeller hub and nose section of the XP-39 over the Model 4 proposal.

The first Airacobra, the prototype XP-39 or Bell Model 11 as it was now known, was given the military aircraft serial number 38-326. It was all metal construction except for its fabric covered control surfaces on the fuselage's rudder and elevators, and the wing's ailerons. It outwardly resembled production P-39s, except most noticeably for its high-sitting, rather bulbous canopy. The prototype was unveiled at Bell's Buffalo plant in March 1938. At the direction of the Army Air Corps, the prototype was powered by a 1,150 horsepower Allison V-1710-17 liquid-cooled inline engine fitted with a B-5 turbo-supercharger on the left side of its fuselage behind the exhaust stacks or outlets behind the cockpit. By comparison, most automobiles today are powered by engines developing less than 300 horsepower. A Curtiss Electric three-bladed propeller made by the Curtiss-Wright Corporation was used. The radiator and oil cooler were on the right side of the fuselage behind the exhaust outlets. The plane was left in a silver natural metal finish except for a dark anti-glare panel painted between the forward canopy and the propeller to prevent sun glare in the pilot's eyes. The vertical tail surfaces had painted horizontal American red and white stripes that were typical of military aviation of that prewar era. The XP-39 was unarmed because the 37mm cannon was not available by that date, but it had the space within its upper forward fuselage for two .50 calibre machine guns and a single 25mm cannon that could fire through the propeller shaft. On December 2, 1938, the 25mm cannon was changed to the new belt-fed 37mm Oldsmobile T-9 cannon described earlier with 20 shells, although as noted, the prototype flew without armament. The 37mm cannon was not delivered until April 30, 1939. The wingspan of the prototype was 35'10", and the length of the fuselage was 28'8".

By 1938, the 8th Pursuit Group received Curtiss P-36 pursuit monoplanes—single-wing fighter planes equipped with a radial engine and a retractable landing gear.

A highly retouched factory photo of the prototype XP-39 taken at Buffalo on Dec. 15, 1938. The prototype was dismantled and taken to Wright Field later that month to be test flown. BELL AIRCRAFT CORP. VIA TRUMAN A. PARTRIDGE, SR.

The History of the Allison V-1710 Engine

Before World War Two, Allison Engines was better known as the Allison Division of General Motors Corporation, the same company that was parent to Cadillac, Packard Electric, Delco-Remy, A.C. Spark Plugs and others. General Motors purchased Allison in 1935, intending to seriously develop the 1710 liquid-cooled engine for both military and civilian aviation markets. The military sales increased, but the civilian and commercial market never developed. The engine was called the 1710 because it possessed a 1,710 cubic inch displacement, roughly five or six times larger than most of today's private automobiles. A typical Allison engine was assembled from over 7,000 parts and required approximately 70,000 inspection checks before the engine was shipped. Allison was headquartered in Indianapolis, Indiana. It produced high-performance liquid-cooled aircraft engines, reaction-propulsion units, and aircraft engine bearings used in all makes of aviation engines.

The design of the Allison V-1710 twelve cylinder liquid-cooled Vee-shaped engine first began in 1930. The first V-1710-A appeared in 1932 developing 750 horsepower. The V-1710-B was used to propel many lighter-than-air or blimp Navy airships. By 1935, the -C engine appeared, developing 1,000 horsepower, and by 1937, a V-1710-C10 was installed in the experimental Curtiss XP-37 fighter plane using a turbo-supercharger. Allison developed the V-1710-D and -E engines specifically for Bell Aircraft Corporation. The -D was used in the Airacuda, but the V-1710-E could drive a propeller through an extension shaft and reduction gearbox as used in the XP-39. Later engine models developed higher power with more streamlined designs possessing less frontal area. The most advanced Allison engine used in the last few Airacobra designs was the V-1710-E19 which weighed 1,435 pounds. Allison V-1710 inline engines, depending on the sub-type, were also developed for P-38s, P-40s, P-63s and early models of the P-51 until the Mustang was converted to American-licensed Packard-built Rolls Royce Merlin engines (both these Allison V-1710 engines and the Merlin were inline engines, whereas the later P-47 used a large radial engine). By the end of the war, some Allison V-1710 engines, such as the -E21 with a turbo-supercharger, developed up to 1,825 horsepower. Allison further developed a series of 24 cylinder Vee-shaped engines that developed an incredible 2,600 horsepower!

Larry Bell Visits European Aircraft Factories

On July 15, 1938, Larry Bell went to Europe to tour military production facilities at the request of President Roosevelt. The President wanted reports of war preparations being made by England, Germany, France and Italy. After touring factories in each country, Mr. Bell reported his findings. He rated Germany as the strongest manufacturer of military aircraft, England as being about half as prepared, and France the least. In his estimation, Germany could produce 8,000 to 10,000 warplanes annually, but cited England as ill-prepared to increase its new aircraft production. From this he recommended the U.S. not make the same mistakes. Larry Bell's conclusions went to President Roosevelt, which contributed to a reassessment of our nation's defense production. Mr. Bell soon stressed productivity at Bell Aircraft. His push for preparedness did not end until the war was won in 1945. Some production methods demonstrated in Germany were incorporated in the Bell plants assembling P-39s.

P-39 Flight Testing Begins

During World War Two, Wright Field at Dayton, Ohio (now Wright-Patterson Air Force Base, also the home of the Air Force Museum) was the headquarters for the Army Air Corps' Materiel Command. This agency was responsible for conceiving, experimenting, testing, ordering, inspecting and supervising all new aircraft, engines, equipment and accessories used by the Army Air Corps. Materiel Command developed prototype equipment until it was ready for mass production. It was then responsible for all equipment purchases used by the Army Air Corps.

With great caution, the prototype XP-39 was delivered to Wright Field by December 27, 1938, in an unassembled condition. More than three months were spent testing and correcting the prototype in preparation for its first flight. Larry Bell and members of the design staff made frequent visits to Dayton to inspect the XP-39's assembly and confer on problems. Taxiing tests began in early March 1939 after solving a series of assembly, engine and fuel tank leakage problems. The prototype's engine was removed on March 8 for changes at Allison. New oil cooler cowlings and tests on the landing gear system followed after extensive ground handling taxi tests. On March 25, the turbo-supercharger was installed. The Allison engine was test run during the last week of March and reinstalled in the XP-39 by April 4. Bell test pilot James Taylor (United States Naval Reserve) returned to Wright Field that day after visiting the prototype several times during its assembly. On April 5, the XP-39's engine ran up to 2700 r.p.m., but it ran somewhat rough between 570 to 1400 r.p.m. without a smooth idle. Only 2650 r.p.m. could be reached in ground running. James Taylor taxied the prototype for ten minutes, but returned to have the brakes adjusted.

The XP-39 flew for twenty minutes on April 6, 1939, at the hands of James Taylor. The only problems noted were "some oil cooler trouble" and the need to adjust the idle setting. The crewchief was Bell's John L. "Mickey" McCarthy. With a normal gross weight of 5,550 pounds, the XP-39 achieved the incredible speed of 390 miles per hour at 20,000 feet and reached it in five minutes during its flight trials. This was a superior speed increase when compared to the P-36's 310 mph. Some minor engine and oil cooling problems were corrected, requiring temporary radiator and oil cooler scoops, and the turbo-supercharger intake was enlarged. In the original design specifications, to assist in more rapid takeoffs, Bell had proposed installing a rocket-powered device to increase takeoff to a rate of climb in excess of 7,500 feet per minute, but this installation was not permitted by the Army Air Corps. The flight tests, however, were a success. Because of the excellent results, the Army Air Force placed contract number AC12635 on April 27, 1939, for twelve preproduction test Bell Model 12 YP-39s and one YP-39A (serial numbers 40-27 through 40-39). These thirteen preproduction aircraft were almost identical to the XP-39 prototype except for some equipment changes. They had two additional .30 calibre machine guns added in their upper forward fuselages. The YP-39A, serial number 40-39, was to test the new design's high-altitude capability using an altitude-rated Allison V-1710-31 engine.

The XP-39 was next transferred to the National Advisory Committee for Aeronautics, or NACA, located at Langley Field, Virginia. The NACA conducted full-scale experimental wind tunnel tests with the prototype. At the end, NACA recommended several modifications for production Airacobras:

1. The wheel doors were more streamlined.
2. A lower streamlined canopy was added.
3. The carburetor air scoop was moved from the left side of the fuselage to behind the canopy.
4. The radiators went from the fuselage sides to the central wing root leading edges.
5. The engine was changed to an Allison V-1710-39 rated at 1,090 horsepower at 13,300 feet. This was a more reliable engine and easier to maintain. It performed well at low and medium altitudes.
6. The turbo-supercharger was deleted from the prototype and the P-39 program.

The modified XP-39 at Wright Field during flight testing in 1939. Note the three-part nosegear doors, which were later changed at NACA's recommendation. BELL AIRCRAFT CORP. VIA TRUMAN A. PARTRIDGE, SR.

The prototype on Nov. 20, 1939, with the NACA changes. The carburetor intake is behind the reduced canopy, and the cleaned-up gear doors are plainly seen. Larry Bell stands at right. BELL AIRCRAFT CORP. VIA TRUMAN A. PARTRIDGE, SR.

It is worth expanding on the last point. If any individual change can be identified from a historical 20/20 clear perspective as being the P-39's primary limiting flaw, it is surely *the removal of the turbo-supercharger* from the P-39's Allison engine for the rest of its career. This reduced the P-39's high-altitude performance drastically, and limited its usable military service in later combat roles. This deletion directly reflected the military philosophy of the late 1930s wherein pursuit planes would be used as low-altitude, close-support aircraft for the Army's ground forces, and not as high-altitude interceptors. The P-39, therefore, suffered from poor planning by the government, not poor design by Bell. *The Airacobra has been the subject of much abuse because of this decision, and it was not the P-39's nor Bell's fault.* The P-39 fully performed the mission it was assigned. Yet had it retained its turbo-supercharger, it could have undertaken the high-altitude interceptor role during the latter part of World War Two.

Because of NACA's tests, Bell modified the XP-39. The prototype was dismantled and rebuilt according to NACA's recommendations. Bell also added improved vertical tail surfaces and installed the guns in the prototype Airacobra. Empty weight rose from 3,995 to 4,530 pounds, and normal gross weight was now 5,834 pounds. The wingspan of the prototype was decreased to 34′, but the length was increased to 29′9″. The height of the airplane stood 11′10″. These changes improved lateral stability.

During the summer of 1939, the 36th Pursuit Squadron of the 8th Pursuit Group tested the experimental Curtiss YP-37, the first pursuit airplane equipped with the new Allison inline engine now rated at 1,000 horsepower. The YP-37's design was based on the P-36. The YP-37 was capable of speeds in excess of 300 miles per hour. Its successor, however, was the legendary Curtiss P-40.

The XP-39A And The XP-39B

After being rebuilt, the prototype was redesignated XP-39B, with "XP-39A" never being allocated. The XP-39B resumed flight testing on November 25, 1939. The NACA changes made the Airacobra more maneuverable at lower altitude, but the maximum speed of 390 miles per hour fell to 375 at 15,000 feet, and the rate of climb decreased to seven and a half minutes to reach 20,000 feet. When the tests were concluded, the modifications were passed to the thirteen YP-39 preproduction Airacobras. Without their turbo-superchargers, the P-39s were somewhat easier to build and maintain in the field. These were perhaps the only tangible benefits derived from deleting the units.

Flight testing the prototype XP-39B began again on Nov. 25, 1939. This photo was taken two weeks later. The prototype still had no armament at this time. BELL AIRCRAFT CORP. VIA TRUMAN A. PARTRIDGE, SR.

The XP-39B during flight testing on Dec. 18, 1939. The central wing radiator intakes are clearly seen. BELL AIRCRAFT CORP. VIA TRUMAN A. PARTRIDGE, SR.

The prototype at Buffalo on Jan. 3, 1940, three days before it was nearly lost when its tricycle gear failed to extend. BELL AIRCRAFT CORP. VIA TRUMAN A. PARTRIDGE, SR.

Bell Displays The P-39 To The Military

On January 6, 1940, Bell Aircraft entertained numerous visitors from the military at Buffalo Airport. Bell showed the first Airacobra, the XP-39. Later the guests were invited to watch Army Air Corps pilot Captain George E. Price fly an aerial demonstration with the Airacobra. Captain Price was with the Production Engineering Division at Wright Field. He was the project officer assigned to Bell for the P-39. After flying a stunning air show which included low passes over the field in excess of 300 miles per hour, Captain Price prepared to land. The tricycle landing gear, however, would not extend. The two wing landing gears held partially open whereas the nose strut did not extend at all. The Captain repeatedly tried emergency procedures, but to no avail. Larry Bell personally ordered the Captain to bail out. He refused and instead executed a slow belly landing smoothly onto the field. The only damage was some de-skinning of the belly and wing sheet metal, and a bent propeller. A problem with a worm gear in the landing system had caused the gear-up problem. This snag was soon corrected. Thirteen days later, Captain Price flew the repaired XP-39 at an aerial demonstration at Bolling Field near Washington, D.C. On September 24, 1940, Captain Price received the Distinguished Flying Cross for his courage while landing the prototype earlier at Buffalo.

The YP-39 Airacobras

All YP-39s were modified in January 1940 with the changes from the prototype Airacobra. The single YP-39A was not modified for high-altitude testing and was instead delivered as a YP-39. The Army Air Corps was still not convinced that high-altitude capability was needed. All thirteen YP-39s were fitted with non-turbo-supercharged Allison V-1710-37 engines developing 1,090 horsepower. Each had full armament consisting of one 37mm cannon firing through the propeller hub with 15 rounds (cannon shells), two .50 calibre M-2 machine guns with 200 rounds (bullets) per gun, and two .30 calibre machine guns with 500 rounds per gun, with all four guns located in the upper forward fuselage above the cannon. The YP-39s were now the deadliest pursuit aircraft ever assembled in the United States. Empty weight of the Airacobra increased to 5,042 pounds, but some pilot armor protection was added in the cockpit. The first YP-39, serial number 40-27, flew on September 13, 1940. Unfortunately, the maximum speed of the YP-39, while fully armed, fell to 368 miles per hour at 15,000 feet.

On October 12, 1940, Captain George E. Price, the pilot who saved the XP-39 on January 6, 1940, took delivery of the first production P-39 for the Army Air Corps.

The prototype modified with a nose cannon for firing tests in fall 1940. Note the missing main gear doors.
BELL AIRCRAFT CORP. VIA TRUMAN A. PARTRIDGE, SR.

The XP-39B and the YP-39s were brought up to the same standards. The nose cannon and machine guns are clearly seen. BELL AIRCRAFT CORP. VIA TRUMAN A. PARTRIDGE, SR.

The service test YP-39s first flew on Sept. 13, 1940, when serial number 40-27 took to the air. This is one of them. BELL AIRCRAFT CORP. VIA TRUMAN A. PARTRIDGE, SR.

When fully armed, the top speed of the YP-39s fell from 375 to 368 miles at 15,000 feet. BELL AIRCRAFT CORP. VIA TRUMAN A. PARTRIDGE, SR.

Gear down, flaps down—a YP-39 on final approach.
BELL AIRCRAFT CORP. VIA TRUMAN A. PARTRIDGE, SR.

An Analysis of the Airacobra's Design

When Bell was certain the Airacobra would go into production, they made it suitable for mass production techniques using many sub-assemblies. Redesigning the P-39 by having designers confer with builders, Bell developed production techniques that were unique in their day. Bell proudly noted in its advertising that the P-39 went "from the experimental stages to mass production in less than 300 days." The Airacobra was divided into five major assemblies for the purpose of design and construction: forward fuselage, rear monocoque fuselage (meaning the assembly was essentially a series of bulkheads with an outer metal skin to give it its structure and shape), outer wing panels, fuselage carry-through member for the wings, and pilot's cabin. Next were major sub-assemblies for the other areas, such as doors and control surfaces. Each sub-assembly was designed as a complete unit to be interchangeable with others. The Airacobra was assembled from 9,000 parts, 54,000 rivets and 1,500 feet of wiring, all put together in a production line process.

The fuselage of the P-39 was made from two sections, a forward fuselage and a rear fuselage. Both were assembled separately and later joined. The forward fuselage stopped behind the engine bay. It contained the wing center section, engine extension shaft, propeller reduction gears, nose landing gear, and various other sub-assemblies. This forward section was based on two built-up aluminum cradle-shaped beams. To it were attached aluminum bulkheads or preshaped inner assemblies, and then the outer aluminum sheet. The pilot's cabin, a separate assembly, was later attached to the forward fuselage. The separate rear fuselage was a semi-monocoque design with eight bulkheads within it. The rear fuselage contained the tail control surfaces and radio equipment.

The two fuselage halves were next spliced together. The nose cowling and forward fuselage contained access doors. The wing's center section was designed as an integral part of the forward fuselage. Outer wing panels were then joined to the wing center section. Each wing panel contained three spars or beam-like structures and ten ribs, all made of aluminum. Each wing panel contained the machine gun compartments and ammunition boxes, a main landing gear well and six self-sealing fuel cells which used a rubberized lining that, when penetrated (by a bullet, for example), would swell up to seal the hole and prevent gas leakage. The wing panels were covered with aluminum sheet flush-riveted smooth to the inner structures. The ailerons or wing control panels were fabric covered and dope treated to shrink and seal the fabric for painting. The split trailing edge flaps, which were the control surfaces used to slow the airplane on landing or takeoff by creating more lift in the wing, formed the lower rear surface of the outer wing panels. They were operated by a one-half horsepower electric motor. They were fully extended or lowered at forty-five degrees with an airspeed of no more than 150 miles per hour. The horizontal and vertical tail surfaces' inner structures were formed from aluminum sheet. The elevators and rudder assemblies were fabric-covered like the ailerons.

The pilot's cabin contained six transparent glass and plexiglas panels attached to the aluminum structure. The cockpit was made up of two assemblies, a permanent forward cabin for the pilot, and a removable rear cabin enclosure covering the engine behind the cabin. Both cockpit doors were made of aluminum and used automobile styling. The doors were made under sub-contract by the Hudson Motor Car Company, an automobile manufacturer that was consolidated into American Motors in the early 1950s, now a part of Chrysler Corporation. Each door had a roll-up window with an emergency door release handle that allowed the pilot to push the door away. The aluminum alloy instrument panel with sub-panels to its right and left housed 36 instruments and sets of switches. The metal bucket seat for the pilot was not adjustable. A type B-11 Sutton safety harness was attached to the seat. The cockpit was designed to accommodate a pilot who was five feet eight inches tall weighing 200 pounds with parachute. The rear cabin was covered with plexiglas and held some of the P-39's radio equipment.

The P-39 was equipped with a fully retractable tricycle landing gear. The nosewheel was self-castering but non-steerable. Extensive testing had been done by Bell earlier on the Airacuda program to control shimmy problems in the nosewheel, and these results were also used in the P-39's design. All three struts were elevated by a 24 volt, three-quarter horsepower electric motor driving the assembly. In an emergency, the landing gear could be hand cranked down into position. The wheels were made of magnesium alloy. The nosewheel diameter was 19 inches, and the main wheels were 26 inches. The nosewheel strut was covered by two side doors when retracted, and the main landing gears by three door sections per strut.

The Allison engine was secured to the forward fuselage half by four pairs of bolts and nuts. The propeller reduction gear box was bolted to the forward bulkhead and connected to the engine by a ten foot long driveshaft running under the pilot's seat. The reduction gearbox had its own separate oiling system. The engine exhaust stacks were made of stainless steel. The P-39 contained a 13.8 gallon oil tank located in the rear fuselage half behind the engine with oil coolers in each outer wing panel. The engine was cooled by a liquid cooling system. The radiator was located below the engine in the rear of the wing's center section. Four air ducts to the radiator were located on the P-39 at the wing center section's leading edge. The Airacobra's battery was located in the forward fuselage beneath the .50 calibre machine guns behind the reduction gear box. The fuse panel was located within the nose gear well on the left side. An electrically operated engine starter was used to start the P-39's engine. The electrical system had an engine-driven generator located on the rear of the Allison engine. The left outer wing panel contained a retractable landing light. The P-39 could de-ice its windshield and propeller by means of a glycol tank antifreeze spray system in the forward fuselage. The elevators were controlled by a tube assembly attached to the control stick which operated to a duplicate cable and pulley system in the rear fuselage. A similar system controlled the wing's ailerons. The rudder was controlled by a system of cables on pulleys only. All fabric covered control surfaces, except the right elevator, had adjustable trim tabs which had control knobs in the left side of the cockpit.

The nose cannon was located on the fuselage centerline and fired through the reduction gear box and propeller hub. The two .50 calibre Type M-2 machine guns in the forward fuselage were synchronized to fire through the propeller arc. Each had flame suppressor blast tubes. Both had ejection chutes to hold spent bullet casings. The empty cannon shells were also contained in the forward fuselage. The wing .30 calibre machine guns' empty shells in later model Airacobras were released into the air through four small doors in the lower wing panels. The P-39 used a combination of steel plate, face-hardened steel plate, and bullet-proof glass to armor itself. Steel plate protected the nose reduction gear box from forward enemy fire. It was also used between the cockpit and the gun compartment. An armor plate was added at the lower base of the forward canopy. An armor bulkhead was immediately located between the engine and the pilot, as a face-hardened steel plate that was mounted behind the oil tank in the rear fuselage. A one and a half inch thick piece of bullet-proof glass was mounted inside the forward section of the canopy ahead of the gun sight, and finally, a two and a half inch thick piece of armor glass was located behind the pilot's seat but ahead of the rear plexiglas canopy.

The First Production Airacobra, The P-39C

One month before the YP-39 flew, the Army Air Corps placed an order for 80 Bell Model 13 Airacobras under contract AC 13383. The Model 13 was the first true production model, generally referred to as the P-39C, although it was briefly referred to as the P-45. The P-39C was powered by an Allison V-1710-35 engine. Its production began in 1940, but these Airacobras were not considered combat-ready aircraft as they did not have self-sealing tanks to minimize fuel leakage if hit by enemy fire, nor defensive armor. They were identical to the YP-39 preproduction Airacobras. On September 14, 1940, the initial order for 80 P-39Cs was changed to add self-sealing fuel tanks. These tanks, however, reduced internal fuel capacity from 170 U.S. gallons to 120 U.S. gallons, although the P-39Cs could carry a 75 U.S. gallon externally mounted drop tank on the centerline beneath the wing that could be released in flight, if needed. As an alternative, a bomb of up to 500 pounds could be carried. The first P-39C, serial number 40-2971, flew in January 1941.

During November 1940, the Army Air Corps conducted accelerated firing tests of the P-39's armament. Three Army pilots, Captains Colman, Price and Swofford, alternately flew over Lake Ontario in a production P-39 taken from the assembly line. They fired 40,000 machine gun bullets and 500 37mm cannon shells over a one week period. The cannon displayed great accuracy. On November 27, 1940, the War Department announced the firing tests provided satisfactory results.

In November 1940, the 8th Pursuit Group moved to Mitchel Field on Long Island in New York.

On November 2, 1940, President Roosevelt toured the Bell assembly plant. A P-39 was quickly put together to give the appearance of a complete Airacobra for the President's visit when in truth there was no Allison engine in the airframe!

In December 1940, Bell Aircraft Corporation began publishing an internal information magazine called *The Bellringer.* The stylish 8½ by 11 inch multi-color monthly publication ran 16 to 20 pages. It was filled with numerous interesting interviews, production technique reports and employee-related news items. *The Bellringer* was continuously published until Volume 5, Number 10 in December 1945.

The P-39C was the first true production Airacobra, although it was practically identical to the YP-39. The first P-39C, 40-2971, flew in January 1941.
BELL AIRCRAFT CORP. VIA TRUMAN A. PARTRIDGE, SR.

The P-39D

Only 20 of the 80 P-39Cs were assembled when the 21st and subsequent Airacobras became P-39Ds. The P-39Cs used serial numbers 40-2971 through 40-2990. Three went to Great Britain under Lend-Lease. Deliveries of the remaining P-39Cs to the Army Air Corps began in January 1941. No P-39C Airacobras, however, ever saw combat duty.

By February 1, the 31st Pursuit Group was made up of the 39th, 40th and 41st Pursuit Squadrons. It was based at Selfridge Field, Michigan under the command of Major John R. Hawkins. The 39th Pursuit Squadron became the first Army Air Corps unit equipped with the new P-39s while commanded by Lieutenant Marvin McNickle. The 39th was further divided into three flights. Gunnery practice was flown over Lake Huron. The 31st Pursuit Group participated in the "Carolina Maneuvers" from September to November 1941. During those maneuvers, five different squadrons flew Airacobras. They maintained an 85 percent availability for flight during the war games which turned in 3,500 flying hours. The 31st later flew P-39s in combat in the South Pacific.

In February 1941, Bell formed its Aircraft Training Course to develop more skilled craftsmen for the aircraft industry to try to double the number of skilled employees. The goal was to develop semi-skilled mechanics after two to eight weeks training depending on the strengths of the trainees. The training was a combination of classroom and in-factory work with instructors. The first director was George B. Fuller.

Between February 12 and March 21, 1941, twenty-seven Army Air Corps pilots from Patterson, Selfridge and Wright Fields flew three Airacobras over 160 accelerated service test hours at Patterson Field in Osborne, Ohio. These tests were run in poor weather, low temperatures and altitudes up to 30,000 feet. The final test results were good. The three Airacobras were next delivered to Selfridge Field, Michigan for active service.

In March 1941, Bell test pilot Vance Breese dove an Airacobra 15,000 feet to pass the final Army Air Corps test at Buffalo. The P-39 also met the Army's positive and negative acceleration requirements. These

The 39th Pursuit Squadron at the Carolina Maneuvers in fall 1941. P-39s flew with an 85 percent availability during this prewar military exercise. BELL AIRCRAFT CORP. VIA TRUMAN A. PARTRIDGE, SR.

The 39th Pursuit Squadron of the 31st Pursuit Group was the first Army Air Corps unit to receive the new P-39 on Feb. 1, 1941, while based at Selfridge Field, Michigan. BELL AIRCRAFT CORP. VIA TRUMAN A. PARTRIDGE, SR.

tests showed the stress the P-39 could handle when making quick directional changes. Vance Breese was one of the most famous test pilots of the late 1930s and 1940s. Earlier, on October 26, 1940, he flew the prototype P-51 Mustang on its first flight for North American Aviation.

The Export Airacobra, The Bell Model 14

While the YP-39 and the P-39C were being flown, Bell Aircraft also developed an export version of the P-39. The Bell Model 14 was similar to the "American" P-39. It was powered by a 1,150 horsepower Allison V-1710-E4 engine which had twelve exhaust stacks on each side instead of the usual six, with the "E" designating it as an "export" version. France ordered 200 Model 14s on October 8, 1939. This was Bell's first large production order valued at $9 million. The order was arranged through the Anglo-French Purchasing Board by Britisher Sir Henry Self in New York City. The deal allowed $2 million in up-front money to keep Bell Aircraft solvent after the shortcomings of the Airacuda program. When France fell to the Germans, Great Britain took the order. Instead of being painted in the usual P-39 olive drab and pale grey colors, the Bell Model 14, later known as the P-400 in the United States, was trimmed in British three-color camouflage. Armament in the P-400 was different. The mixture and propeller controls on the throttle quadrant were reversed from the standard P-39. The slower firing 37mm cannon was replaced by the faster and more reliable 20mm Hispano Suiza M1 cannon with 60 rounds. The P-400 was equipped instead with six .303 Browning machine

Bell company aircraft NX-BA14 was a research Airacobra used in the development of the export Model 14, the British Airacobra I. It had self-sealing fuel tanks and armor plate. Photo taken in early 1940. BELL AIRCRAFT CORP. VIA TRUMAN A. PARTRIDGE, SR.

A Bell research Model 14 Airacobra in early 1940. BELL AIRCRAFT CORP. VIA TRUMAN A. PARTRIDGE, SR.

guns. British radio equipment was added as well as an oxygen system using different pressure.

The Airacobra In British Service

In spring 1940, before the advent of the famed Battle of Britain, the British were in dire need of fighter planes. There were no P-47s nor P-51s, and the supply of British Hurricane and Spitfire fighters at home was not adequate. On April 12, 1940, under three different orders, A-218, A-1326 and A-1476, the British ordered 675 of Bell's Model 14 export fighters for the Royal Air Force, or RAF, under Bell Detail Specification Report Number 14-945-001, Revision 6. The British renamed the plane the Caribou. The first Model 14 was shipped in May 1941 but did not arrive in England until July 3, 1941. The British renamed it the Airacobra I. The first British Airacobra flew three days later. During its flight trials, the Model 14's relative performance was inferior for the British. The maximum speed contended by Bell at 400 miles per hour was never achieved, actually falling short by 33 miles per hour. This lower speed was a problem for the RAF because opposing German Bf-109Fs, introduced in the German Air Force, the Luftwaffe, in January 1941, were achieving 390 miles per hour at altitude and actually outperforming the British Spitfires. Bell admitted their top speed of 400 miles per hour came from a highly polished Airacobra weighing a ton less than the export Model 14. When flown against British Spitfires and Hurricanes, the Model 14 was inferior in climbing rate and service ceiling. It could not be easily flown from some smaller British air fields. The nose guns built up carbon monoxide fumes in the cabin when fired, and the armament was difficult to access. Despite these shortcomings, the British allocated eleven Airacobras to No. 601 Squadron of the Royal Auxiliary Air Force located at an RAF base at Manston at the end of September 1941. No. 601 Squadron turned in their Hawker Hurricanes for the

A Bell Model 14 export Airacobra I with twelve exhaust stacks on each side indicating a V-1710-E "export" Allison engine. No British serial number, however, has been applied.
BELL AIRCRAFT CORP. VIA TRUMAN A. PARTRIDGE, SR.

A Bell Model 14 Airacobra I on the ramp at Buffalo. This was mostly likely a test model as it has neither a British serial number nor the twelve exhaust stacks per side denoting an export Allison engine.
BELL AIRCRAFT CORP. VIA TRUMAN A. PARTRIDGE, SR.

An Airacobra I in flight over Buffalo. The export Model 14 carried six .303 Browning machine guns with two housed in the nose and two contained in each outer wing's leading edge.
BELL AIRCRAFT CORP. VIA TRUMAN A. PARTRIDGE, SR.

An Airacobra I on test flight over Buffalo.
BELL AIRCRAFT CORP. VIA TRUMAN A. PARTRIDGE, SR.

new Airacobras. On October 9, No. 601 Squadron flew four Airacobras on a strafing mission to the French coast. The need for further changes to the British Airacobras and minimal spare parts soon led to many Airacobras not being serviceable. Four Airacobras later crashed with two British pilots killed. No additional air operations were flown as the British rejected the Airacobra as unsuitable. All Model 14s were withdrawn from front line service by December 1941, despite Bell engineers advising the British they had not properly ballasted their Airacobras to obtain the correct balance. A third Airacobra pilot was killed on February 13, 1942, after an unrecoverable flat spin. From the 675 export Model 14 Airacobras for the RAF, only eight were accepted, 212 were rerouted to the Soviet Union, 179 were recovered for U.S. service and renamed the P-400 and used in the fighting in the South Pacific, and 54 were lost at sea after German submarine attacks. The P-400s used by the American forces maintained their British serial numbers and three-color camouflage. Because the P-400s had a different oxygen system pressure valve, they were difficult for American crewchiefs to service in the combat theatre.

Bell test pilot Bob Stanley prepares an Airacobra I for flight. All Model 14s used British serial numbers, even when later returned to the United States Army Air Corps. The 20mm cannon is clearly seen in the propeller hub. BELL AIRCRAFT CORP. VIA TRUMAN A. PARTRIDGE, SR.

Bell test pilot Bob Stanley lines up Airacobra I AH 621 for the camera. This aircraft does not have an export engine as seen by the six exhaust outlets on each side. BELL AIRCRAFT CORP. VIA TRUMAN A. PARTRIDGE, SR.

Bell Aircraft Corporation was always looking for ways to improve its Airacobra. This P-39C tested a four-bladed propeller later found on some late P-39Qs and all P-63s. Photo most likely taken at Wright Field as there are P-40s in the background.
BELL AIRCRAFT CORP. VIA TRUMAN A. PARTRIDGE, SR.

Another test P-39, possibly with a supercharger. Photo taken Sept. 6, 1941.
BELL AIRCRAFT CORP. VIA TRUMAN A. PARTRIDGE, SR.

Still another test Airacobra. Unknown serial number, but most likely a P-39C or P-39D. Photo circa fall 1941.
BELL AIRCRAFT CORP. VIA TRUMAN A. PARTRIDGE, SR.

Several test P-39s parked forward with many others waiting for propellers at Bell. Photo most likely from 1941. BELL AIRCRAFT CORP. VIA TRUMAN A. PARTRIDGE, SR.

Bell's P-39 Sets A Speed Record

On January 8, 1941, Bell Aircraft attempted a new world speed record with an Airacobra. On that morning, Lieutenant Andrew C. McDonough, another Naval Reserve Officer, climbed a company P-39 to 27,000 feet. He then dove 21,000 feet under power. His Airacobra's instruments recorded a maximum speed of 620 miles per hour. Although the test was explained to show the reliability of the P-39's structure, the attention given Bell by the press didn't hurt from a public relations standpoint!

The First American Airacobras Enter Combat

The P-39D, or Bell Model 15, was the first Airacobra to see combat. The remaining 60 P-39Cs noted earlier, serial numbers 40-2991 through 40-3050, became P-39Ds, along with an additional 344 Airacobras under contract AC 15675 placed on September 13, 1940. These were serial numbers 41-6722 through 41-7052, 41-7057 and 41-7058, and 41-7080 through 41-7115. All P-39Ds were powered by 1,150 horsepower Allison V-1710-35 engines with a different 10'5" Curtiss Electric propeller. The fuselage length increased to 30'2". The weight was now 5,462 pounds empty, and the service ceiling was 32,100 feet. P-39Ds carried a 37mm nose cannon with 30 rounds, four wing mounted .30 calibre machine guns with 1,000 rounds per gun, and two .50 calibre nose machine guns with 200 rounds per gun. The P-39D could also carry one 250-lb., 325-lb. or 500-lb. bomb. Despite these improvements, the maximum speed dropped to 360 miles per hour at 15,000 feet, and the fighter performed poorly at higher altitudes. The first P-39Ds entered Army Air Corps service in February 1941.

The legendary 56th Fighter Group, which flew P-47 Thunderbolts over France and Germany under the leadership of Colonel Hub Zemke, was earlier based at Mitchel Field, New York and flew in defense of the city. The 56th Pursuit Group flew a combination of P-39s, P-400s and P-40s while training its members. In June 1942, the 56th Fighter Group became the first outfit to receive the new Republic P-47 fighter plane when Hub Zemke took command. By the end of the war, the 56th's total of enemy aircraft destroyed was the highest of any American fighter group flying in Europe.

P-39Ds on Bell's assembly line in 1940. These Airacobras entered Army Air Corps service in February 1941.
BELL AIRCRAFT CORP. VIA TRUMAN A. PARTRIDGE, SR.

P-39Ds in final assembly in an extremely clean Bell factory. The "D" was the first Airacobra to see combat.
BELL AIRCRAFT CORP. VIA TRUMAN A. PARTRIDGE, SR.

The Experimental XP-39Es

Another aircraft engine manufacturing company during the war was the Aircraft Engine Division of the Continental Motors Corporation, headquartered at Muskegon, Michigan. Continental Motors was an automobile manufacturer that in 1928 began producing aircraft engines. One of its subsidiaries, the Continental Aviation and Engineering Corporation, spent years developing a high-powered liquid-cooled engine, the I-1430. It was an inverted Vee-shaped design that *was* supercharged. It developed 2,100 horsepower. The I-1430 was installed in many experimental aircraft, including pursuit fighters from Curtiss, Lockheed, McDonnell, and Bell Aircraft Corporation.

On April 10, 1941, two P-39Ds were ordered modified and flight tested under contract AC18373 using this experimental Continental engine. These Airacobras, serial numbers 41-19501 and 41-19502, and a third added on October 27, 1942, 41-71464, were redesignated XP-39E, also known as Bell Model 23. These Airacobras had 35' 10" wingspans and weighed 6,935 pounds empty. When they were assembled, however, the new Continental engines were not adequately developed, and Allison V-1710-47 engines were used instead. These Airacobras were armed the same as the P-39D, but they featured NACA 66 series laminar flow wings with squarely shaped wing tips. These laminar flow wings reduced drag when the air flowed over in layers rather than separating from the wing. Each XP-39E, however, tested different tail surface configurations. One XP-39E was redesignated to P-76, and it almost went into separate production from the P-39s. A maximum speed of 386 miles per hour was achieved at 21,680 feet. Research from the three XP-39Es was used later in the P-63 Kingcobra program at Bell.

Bell Aircraft Expands

By 1940, the Airacuda project was completed and two Airacobras were built. In September 1940, however, Bell received an $8.5 million Emergency Facilities Contract to build another Airacobra assembly plant on a 65-acre area near Niagara Falls Airport outside Buffalo. During 1941 Bell assembled 756 P-39s. On August 25, 1941, Bell received a $75 million contract to assem-

The first Bell Model 23, the XP-39E, seen on March 6, 1942. This Airacobra, 41-19501, had laminar flow wings with different tail surfaces. It looked the most like the later P-63 Kingcobra of the three XP-39Es built. BELL AIRCRAFT CORP. VIA TRUMAN A. PARTRIDGE, SR.

The second XP-39E, 41-19502, during winter 1941-42. The undersized tail surfaces probably lessened stability on this version. BELL AIRCRAFT CORP. VIA TRUMAN A. PARTRIDGE, SR.

The third XP-39E, 41-71464, as seen in late 1942. Note the squarely cut control surface tips, much like those on the P-51 Mustang. BELL AIRCRAFT CORP. VIA TRUMAN A. PARTRIDGE, SR.

ble 2,000 Airacobras for the Army Air Corps, and by 1944, Bell produced twenty Airacobras every day. By January 1940, Bell employed 1,170 people, and this later peaked in February 1944 with 50,674 employees. During the summer of 1942, Bell hired one thousand people every week! In September 1941, Bell formed the Bomber Parts Division after receiving a twelve and a half-million dollar contract to supply elevators, stabilizers and rear gun enclosures for Boeing B-17F four-engine bombers. In January 1942, Bell Aircraft began graduating students from its Service Training School called Camp Cataract. By April 1943, 920 students had graduated. The courses offered were basic school, two-week and refresher courses. The subjects taught were P-39 flying characteristics, field conduct and instructional methods. Bell later added an elementary course in aerodynamics. By July 1943, a nine-day refresher course was added for returning field representatives. On March 30, 1942, ground was broken in Marietta, Georgia for a new Bell B-29 four-engine bomber plant, built under sub-con-

A collection of three-color camouflage Airacobra Is and P-39Fs at Bell on Dec. 23, 1941.
BELL AIRCRAFT CORP. VIA TRUMAN A. PARTRIDGE, SR.

tract to Boeing Aircraft.

On November 1, 1941, Bell Aircraft was awarded a certificate of achievement by the George Washington University Law Department for its successful development and production of the P-39. Larry Bell received the award on behalf of Bell Aircraft Corporation, "as one of the outstanding leaders in defense work, for its success in the development and production of Airacobra cannon-carrying fighter planes."

P-39s Enter Combat On Many Fronts

After the Japanese attack on Pearl Harbor in late 1941 and America's entry into the war, the Army Air Corps had three Pursuit Groups flying the P-39. The 8th Pursuit Group was near New York City. The 16th Pursuit Group was flying P-39Ds defending the Panama Canal Zone, and the 31st Pursuit Group, the first unit receiving the Airacobra, was stationed at Baer Field, Indiana. P-39Ds of the 15th Pursuit Group's 47th Pursuit Squadron were the first Airacobras to become operational in Hawaii on December 21, 1941, flying from Wheeler Field.

Between December 23, 1941, and March 18, 1942, more than 90 P-39s and 100 P-400s along with 337 P-40s arrived in Australia to defend against the Japanese. Of these Airacobras and Warhawks, 125 were lost in combat or due to accidents, 75 were transferred to the Royal Australian Air Force, 74 were being repaired, and about 100 awaited final assembly. By March 18, 1942, only 33 P-39s, 92 P-400s, and 52 P-40s were on strength.

On February 9, 1942, the 70th Pursuit Squadron on Fiji, east of Australia, received its first 25 P-39s. On February 26, the 67th Pursuit Squadron was equipped with 25 P-400s while at Melbourne, Australia. As of March 1942, the 67th was performing P-39 patrols over Tontouta, an old French air field, and Noumea, New Caledonia. The 68th Pursuit Group was established at Amberley Field on the eastern coast of Australia at Brisbane that same month, and soon equipped with P-400s and P-39Ds.

In April 1942, the 31st Pursuit Group, a part of the 8th Air Force, prepared to fly its P-39s to England along with B-17 bombers of the 97th Bomber Group and P-38 fighters of the 1st Pursuit Group. The 31st flew to New England to train in ferrying their planes over the North Atlantic with the B-17s. On June 4, however, the 31st was ordered to England, but without the 97th's B-17s to lead them. The 31st went to England without its Airacobras and transitioned into British Spitfires after arriving. The 31st thus became the first American combat unit in Europe to enter battle flying British fighter planes.

P-39s of the 8th Pursuit Group assisted in the defense of Australia. They were moved by the end of April 1942 to Port Moresby, an advanced refueling field for Australian based bombers, located on the southeast coast of New Guinea, the major island mass northeast of Australia. On April 30, 1942, thirteen of the 26 P-39s from the 35th and 36th Pursuit Squadron flew their first combat mission under Lieutenant Colonel Boyd D. Wagner. The P-39s strafed fuel storage areas and enemy aircraft on the ground at Salamaua and Lae, northeast of Port Moresby on New Guinea. The Airacobras engaged enemy fighters, and one Zero was destroyed by Major George Greene. Four P-39s were lost, however, with three due to hits in their coolant systems. These were the first hits made on enemy aircraft by the Airacobra. Many of Lieutenant Colonel Wagner's pilots lacked adequate training. Equipment and maintenance items were below average. The P-39s initially found it difficult to meet the enemy fighters on equal terms. The Airacobra's toughness, heavy firepower and self-sealing fuel tanks were greatly appreciated by its pilots, but the P-39s were not as maneuverable as the lighter Japanese fighters. The enemy fighters could avoid combat with the P-39s by outclimbing them.

In late May 1942, pilots of the 35th Fighter Group's 40th and 41st Fighter Squadrons arrived with P-400s to relieve the P-39 pilots hard hit by malaria from the 8th Fighter Group (as of May 15, 1942, the term "pursuit" was replaced by "fighter"). On June 9, 1942, the pilots of the 35th Fighter Group shot down five Japanese Zeros over Morobe on New Guinea's northeast coast. In June, the 8th Fighter Group returned to Townsville on Australia's northeast coast. In July, the 35th Fighter Group's 40th Fighter Squadron shot down four Japanese bombers and a Zero over Port Moresby. The 35th Fighter Group had 83 P-400s within its two squadrons as of July 18, 1942, while based at Port Moresby. Prior to this, approximately 20 Airacobras were shot down in combat, eight were lost in forced landings, and three were destroyed while on the ground. On July 21, 1942, the Japanese landed on Buna on the coast of Papua New Guinea due east of Port Moresby, and only the 39th and 40th Fighter Squadrons of the 35th Fighter Group were based at Port Moresby along with several Australian units. The next day the P-39s along with P-400s, P-40s, B-25 and B-26 medium bombers and B-17 heavy bombers attacked the enemy convoy and landing barges. The Airacobras used their heavy firepower on the enemy barges and shore positions. One P-400, several bombers and an Australian P-40 were lost.

On May 31, 1942, the Seventh Air Force on Hawaii had 22 P-39s of which 17 were in commission and on alert ready for a second anticipated attack by the Japanese on the Hawaiian Islands.

On July 17, 1942, the Royal Australian Air Force received ten P-39Fs and twelve P-39Ds from the United States Army Air Force's Fifth Air Force. These Airacobras were at air fields near Sydney, Australia. The RAAF flew their loaned Airacobras until November 1943, but the enemy was never encountered. Three of the P-39Fs were lost in accidents, but the remaining 19 Airacobras were returned to the Fifth Air Force.

On August 8, 1942, 32 P-400s equipped with bomb racks from the 35th Fighter Group flew from Port Moresby to Kokoda across the Owen Stanley Mountains to attack Japanese supply storage areas.

The 67th Fighter Squadron from New Caledonia landed with five P-400s on August 22, 1942 on Guadalcanal, an island east of Port Moresby which was part in the Solomon Islands. The unit was commanded by Captain Dale Brannon. Nine more P-400s led by Captain John Thompson landed five days later. The 67th served with distinction while flying from Henderson Field, a former Japanese air field with the poorest of operating conditions. Many of the 67th's Airacobras sported a painted set of shark's teeth and eyes similar to the American Volunteer Group's P-40s in China. The 67th proved extremely effective, putting the Airacobra's nose cannon to its best use strafing Japanese positions ashore and at sea. On September 5, 1942, two P-400s strafed fifteen Japanese barges, causing severe losses to the 700 soldiers on board and later sinking one of the barges. The P-400s continued their attacks on Japanese ships in the area. The soundness of the P-39's tricycle landing gear was demonstrated by the P-400s on Guadalcanal. The Airacobras were able to take off in the muddy conditions on Henderson Field when other fighters with conventional landing gear were otherwise grounded. During 1943, the 67th moved to Woodlark, an island closer to the Solomon Islands to their northwest. In 1944, after two years of dedicated service, the 67th transitioned into P-38s.

By August 1942, the Japanese were being pushed back. The 35th Fighter Group was flying a collection of P-39Ds, P-400s and some of the later P-39 subvariants, the P-39D-1 and the P-39D-2. The 35th moved up to Tsili-Tsili, and then to Nadzab by October.

On August 26, 1942, six Airacobras of the 80th Fighter Squadron led by Lieutenant William A. Brown raided the Japanese air field at Buna on New Guinea's southern coast. Ten Zeros were surprised while taking off and were shot down. Lieutenants Rogers and Halveston both knocked one down, and Lieutenant Roberts and Lieutenant William A. Brown, their leader, both shot down two. On August 27, P-400s of the 41st Fighter Squadron shot down five more Zeros.

On October 3, 1942, the 347th Fighter Group was activated on New Caledonia, flying both P-39D and P-400 Airacobras.

By November 1942, the 8th Fighter Group began replacing its P-400s with newer P-39Ds. The 68th Fighter Squadron joined the 347th Fighter Group at New Caledonia, an island due east of Australia.

By November 12, 1942, the 339th Fighter Squadron located at Henderson Field on Guadalcanal was operating a mixture of both P-39s and newer P-38s. By December, Colonel Henry Viccellio brought his 70th Fighter Squadron's P-39s to fly with the 339th, both units being part of the 347th Fighter Group. The P-39s were used to bomb and strafe while the P-38s flew patrol. The pilots rotated between the Airacobras and the Lightnings.

Between December 1942 and January 1943, the Japanese attempted building a new air field on Munda in the Solomon Islands northwest of Guadalcanal. On December 6, P-39s attacked trucks, carts and steamrollers at the site. The constant strafing slowed the development of the new field. On December 24, P-39s along with Marine Wildcats and dive bombers caught over twenty Zeros attempting take off. Almost all Japanese planes were destroyed in the air or on the ground with no losses to the American forces.

Between December 1942 and March 1943, P-39s flew escort for A-24 bombers in the southwest Pacific in addition to numerous patrolling and strafing missions.

On February 6, 1943, eight P-39s escorting C-47 cargo transports to Wau attacked 24 enemy aircraft with 11 Zeros and one Japanese Sally bomber claimed destroyed.

P-39D Sub Variants

By late summer 1942, the P-39D-1 appeared in combat. This was the first Airacobra assembled under Lend-Lease contracts, a political means whereby military equipment was given to other countries in return for future payments, although the United States knew it might not receive them. In March 1941, the Congress

This Airacobra, 41-28257, was the first P-39D-1 assembled. The D-1 used a 20mm cannon, two .50 calibre machine guns in the nose, and four wing-mounted .30 calibre machine guns. BELL AIRCRAFT CORP. VIA TRUMAN A. PARTRIDGE, SR.

A P-39D-1 being weighed at Bell to determine its center of gravity. The 20mm cannon is clearly seen.
BELL AIRCRAFT CORP. VIA TRUMAN A. PARTRIDGE, SR.

A test P-39D-1 modified with an oversized vertical fin and what appears to be a long-range belly tank.
BELL AIRCRAFT CORP. VIA TRUMAN A. PARTRIDGE, SR.

of the United States empowered President Roosevelt to send military hardware to other nations whose defense was important to America's survival. The United States supplied equipment to Russia beginning in June 1941. By the end of the war, 7,925 American aircraft were supplied to Russia under Lend-Lease, of which more than half were Airacobras. They were sent to Alaska and then flown across to Siberia and Russia with Russian pilots. Russia lacked the fighter aircraft needed to defend against the invading German air force and army. American-made P-39s filled that void. The Airacobra contributed greatly to the Soviet effort to defeat the German invader. Between September 1942 and March 1943, the Soviet mission located in Fairbanks, Alaska accepted 151 P-39s at Ladd Field. The last Airacobra was accepted by the Russians in September 1944, not long after P-39 production ceased. The last Bell P-63 Kingcobra was turned over in June 1945. The last American plane from any source was delivered to the Soviet mission on September 20, 1945. The majority of these aircraft were fighters made by Bell.

The P-39D-1, or Bell Model 14A, was powered by an Allison V-1710-35 engine. A total of 336 were built under contract AC 32 placed June 11, 1941 and contract AC 156 placed September 17, 1941. P-39D-1s used serial numbers 41-28257 through 41-28406, 41-38220 through 41-38404, and 41-38563. The P-39D-1 was the first to use the newly redesigned small dorsal vertical fin fillet ahead of the rudder that helped stabilize the Airacobra. It became standard and was retrofitted to many earlier P-39Ds. Some P-39D-1s, along with the P-400, were flown by the 347th Fighter Group in August 1942 on Guadalcanal. The P-39D-1 was not a good interceptor, but it excelled as a ground-attack and fighter-bomber aircraft. It featured a 20mm nose cannon, two fuselage .50 calibre machine guns and four wing mounted .30 calibre machine guns.

The P-39D-2, or Bell Model 14A-1, differed only by its more powerful Allison V-1710-63 (E6) engine developing 1,325 horsepower for takeoff with a 2:1 reduction gear at the propeller assembly along with a 37mm cannon. A total of 158 were assembled under contract AC 156 placed June 1, 1942 using serial numbers 41-38405 through 41-38562. All P-39D-2s could carry a 145 U.S. gallon drop tank. Some flew with the 31st Fighter Group in North Africa in 1943. Two other sub-variants were produced. The P-39D-3 and D-4 were D-2s converted for ground-attack roles. They carried armor at their oil and glycol coolers and two cameras in their aft fuselages. They used the V-1710-35 engine. All D-3 and D-4s were flown in combat in Italy.

P-39 Spin Testing

The P-39's spin characteristics became a major concern for many Airacobra pilots. Wright Field sent an urgent telegram to Bell Aircraft requesting a demonstration of the spin recovery of either a P-39D-1 or a P-39D-2 Airacobra after four P-39s in one group had been lost due to the pilots' inability to recover their Airacobras from flat spins. Bell Aircraft conducted a series of nine spin tests during October 1942 using different balance and weight configurations that met or exceeded the Army's requirements. The spin tests were witnessed from the air by the Army Air Force's resident officer. The results were judged adequate, with the test P-39's spin recoveries being "prompt and decisive." It was concluded that no basic deficiencies existed in the Airacobra's design that prohibited recovery from spins. The test results did note the P-39 could be unforgiving in a flat spin if proper spin recovery techniques were not followed. They noted there must be adequate altitude to recover the aircraft as well as having the Airacobra properly loaded for balancing. Despite these results, the NACA published Memorandum Report L-602 in September 1943, entitled "Measurement of the Flying Qualities of a Bell P-39D-1 Airplane," by H. I. Johnson. NACA criticized the Airacobra for: (1) the effectiveness of the ailerons in almost all flying conditions, (2) sudden stalling without any warning, and (3) constantly requiring aircraft trim adjustments.

The Bell Modification Center

Bell developed the Bell Modification Center primarily to modify P-39s flying the northern route to Russia under Lend-Lease. Changes in the oil system, special radios, cameras or other equipment were added. The center also made changes to other aircraft such as Beechcraft C-45 transports, Curtiss P-40s, North American P-51B Mustangs, its own P-63s, Dehavilland Mosquito bombers and the huge PBY Catalina flying boats. A total of 7,300 aircraft passed through the center at a cost of $4,457,000 before the war's end.

Comparing the P-39 with the Japanese Zero

The Zero was the premier fighter aircraft of the Japanese fighting forces throughout the war. It received its name after being designated the A6M1 Type O carrier-borne fighter by the Japanese Navy. The "O" was the last number in the Japanese calendar equivalent for 1940, that being the year 2600 in Japan, the year the new fighter would be in service. The Japanese seldom referred to this fighter as the A6M1, but rather as the "Reisen," or "Type Zero Fighter," or simply the "Zero-sen." Allied intelligence called it the "Zeke," but the term "Zero" was by far the more popular name.

The Zero was a light and highly maneuverable airframe coupled to the best radial engine available. This gave the Japanese an extremely advanced fighter. The Zero was well armed with two 7.7mm machine guns in its upper forward fuselage behind the engine cowling and a 20mm Type 99 cannon in each outer wing beyond the landing gear armed with 60 rounds per gun. This armament gave the American forces a highly potent adversary.

The prototype Zero flew on April 1, 1939, with a top speed of 306 miles per hour. Production Zeros, actually A6M2s with a top speed at 310 miles per hour, joined the Japanese navy in July 1940. They flew in combat over China, and were first used against the United States at Pearl Harbor. The Zero's early successes created a tidal wave of fear among the Allies. The Zero was a new design that met with great success almost immediately in combat, and there was little intelligence gathered on it when World War Two started. There was a seemingly impenetrable veil of fear surrounding the Zero.

The veil, however, was lifted on June 3, 1942. During Japan's attacks on Dutch Harbor in Alaska's Aleutian Islands, Japanese Petty Officer Tadayoshi Koga developed engine trouble while flying his Model 21 A6M2 Zero. He tried to land on Akutan Island in the Aleutians. After lowering his landing gear, he flipped his Zero over on the grassy marsh surface and died in the crash. Five weeks later, the United States Navy surveyed the wreckage and found the Zero repairable. It was disassembled and shipped to the Assembly and Repair Department at Naval Air Station North Island, located at San Diego, California. After the damaged Zero arrived in August 1942, it was repaired for test flying. Despite no repair manuals, extensive nose, canopy and tail damage, and using a nearly identical replacement Hamilton Standard propeller, the newly "Americanized" rebuilt Zero, now painted with American white stars on blue circles, was ready two months later. The Zero was flown against an Army Air Force P-38F, P-40F and an early P-51, as well as a Navy F4F-4 Wildcat and an F4U-1 Corsair to obtain better data. Along with these contemporary American fighters, a Bell P-39D-1 Airacobra was flown against the captured Zero.

Flying against the Zero from a takeoff position in formation, the Airacobra, with 52 inches of manifold pressure, left the Zero behind. The P-39 passed 5,000 feet as the Zero hit 4,000 feet. At 5,000 feet, from a cruise position at 230 miles per hour, the P-39 had better acceleration away from the Zero. While climbing from 5,000 to 10,000 feet at their best climb without the benefit of the zoom effect (diving to gain speed and then pulling up), the P-39 reached 10,000 feet six seconds before the Zero. At 10,000 feet from a cruise at 220 miles per hour, the P-39 could run ahead of the Zero quickly. While climbing from 10,000 feet to 12,500 feet, both fighters, however, were equal. Climbing above 12,500 feet, the Zero outdistanced the Airacobra. Between 15,000 to 20,000 feet, the Zero easily outclassed the P-39. No tests were finished above 20,000 feet. On another test started from takeoff with a straight climb, the P-39 outpaced the Zero until reaching 14,800 feet. Above this altitude, the Zero outclimbed the Airacobra. At 25,000 feet from a cruise at 180 miles per hour, the Zero pulled away from the Airacobra for three lengths and maintained the lead for a minute and a half. Within thirty seconds, however, the P-39 had the lead over the Zero by one length. Neither the early Allison-powered Mustang nor the Warhawk completed their tests against the Zero because of problems with both American planes' Allison engines. The captured Zero, incidentally, was destroyed during summer 1944 when a Navy Helldiver pilot accidentally taxied into it. He cut the Zero to pieces at the tail section behind its rebuilt cockpit.

Japanese Zeros fought the Second World War with outstanding success until the end of 1942. The data from the captured Zero helped void the Zero's air superiority. Fierce fighting with land-based Zeros over northeastern New Guinea occurred during summer 1942 as American forces struck back at the Japanese. Although the Zero was considered superior to the American Airacobras, Warhawks and Wildcats, American pilots had developed the skills necessary to beat the Zero. Americans flying P-39s, P-40s, and F4Fs now fought on equal terms because the Zero was no longer the invincible mystery warrior. By the end of 1942, newer American P-38s, P-47s and P-51s along with Navy F6F Hellcats were able to meet or beat the Zero. Many early Zeros provided inadequate pilot protection with no self-sealing fuel tanks. When the Zero was met on equal terms or bested, few could withstand the return fire. It wasn't until 1944 that better pilot protection was added to production Zeros. By then the lack of skilled Japanese pilots along with the superior speed of the newer American fighters defeated the later but still dangerous Japanese Zero fighters. A true air-superiority

An unidentified P-39F at Buffalo, one of 229 Model 15B Airacobras built. The twelve exhaust stacks on each side can be seen. This photo was taken in 1940 or 1941. BELL AIRCRAFT CORP. VIA TRUMAN A. PARTRIDGE, SR.

replacement fighter for the Zero was never developed in sufficient numbers to affect the outcome of the war.

The P-39F

The next model Airacobra was the P-39F, or Bell Model 15B. The P-39F was nearly identical to the P-39D except the F had twelve exhaust stacks instead of the usual six. An Aeroproducts constant speed propeller with an 11'1" diameter built by General Motors was fitted, replacing the Curtiss Electric prop. A constant speed propeller is one that self-adjusts automatically to airspeed and power changes to keep the r.p.m., or revolutions per minute of the engine, the same. A total of 229 were built under contract AC 15675 placed on September 13, 1940, using serial numbers 41-7116 through 41-7344. Two P-39Fs were modified for photo-reconnaisance work and redesignated P-39F-1s. A further variant, the P-39F-2, was a field modified Airacobra used for ground-support. It had additional protective lower armor and rear fuselage cameras.

The P-39D and F In The Aleutians

Alaska, and the Aleutian Islands, which project to the west from Alaska's southwestern corner, began a rapid military buildup following America's initial defeat at Pearl Harbor. P-40E fighters arrived along with B-26 medium bombers by January 1942 to replace the obsolete P-36 fighters and B-18 medium bombers predominantly used for defense. By February 1942, the Eleventh Air Force was designated for the Alaskan theatre.

In early June 1942, the Japanese launched their first attacks on the Aleutians. By June 24, the first P-39Fs arrived in Alaska to join the defense. The 54th Fighter Group was sent, consisting of the 42nd, 56th and 57th Fighter Squadrons, who had received their Airacobras three months earlier. They arrived at Elmendorf Field in south central Alaska (now Elmendorf Air Force Base). The 57th stayed there, but the 56th was dispatched to Nome in northwestern Alaska, and the 42nd Fighter Squadron to Kodiak in southern Alaska. By late June, the Japanese had a foothold on two of the western Aleutian islands.

The fourth to the last P-39F, 41-7341, at Bell on March 23, 1942. The tail number has been censored out. Bell test pilot Jack Woolams stands in the middle. BELL AIRCRAFT CORP. VIA TRUMAN A. PARTRIDGE, SR.

By August 1942, sixteen P-39Ds, which had previously flown air defense for Kodiak, were flown to the Aleutians. They flew from steel matting covered runways.

On September 14, 1942, the first major bombing mission was flown against the Japanese. Fourteen P-39s flew with P-38s in defense of B-24 bombers and a lone B-17 bomber. Both approached the Japanese positions low over the water to avoid detection. The Airacobras attacked using their 37mm cannons to destroy the Japanese anti-aircraft guns. The P-38s attacked the enemy aircraft, primarily Japanese Rufes, which were floatplane versions of the Zero. The Rufes, however, attacked the P-39s first. Lieutenant Gene L. Arth of the 42nd Fighter Squadron fired into a Jake floatplane fighter, which was a three-place reconnaissance seaplane similar in configuration to a Rufe, which next crashed in the water. Lieutenant Wintow E. Matthews, also of the 42nd, fired on a Rufe which exploded. All Airacobras returned safely. The raid was America's first successful air attack in return on the Japanese in the Aleutians. It was also the turning point in the Aleutians. The weather cleared again by September 25 and another raid, with eleven P-39s in support of B-24s and a single B-17, was flown. A second raid later that day launched 15 P-39s. Both missions were successful with no casualties. On September 28, Captain Arthur T. Rice of the 57th knocked down a Rufe with a single 37mm shell. On October 2, Lieutenant James R. Burgett, III, of the 56th shot down a Rufe as did Captain Kenneth E. George and Lieutenant Cecil A. Thomas, both of the 42nd Fighter Squadron. The next day, Captains Louis H. Bowman and Pat M. Deberry of the 42nd both destroyed a Jake. Another Rufe was destroyed by Lieutenant Frank A. Beagle of the 57th. By the end of 1942, all P-39s were withdrawn from the Aleutians, but of 34 enemy aircraft shot down during the battle which lasted until mid-1943 and for which the P-39s were there for only the first half, ten Japanese planes were credited to the P-39 pilots of the 54th Fighter Group, with the 42nd Fighter Squadron taking six.

P-39s in Europe in 1942

The 31st Fighter Group activated three fighter squadrons. The 307th, 308th and 309th were assigned Airacobras in southern England. Between August and October 1942, the Group escorted bombers to targets inside France and strafed German land and sea targets along the French coast. The 31st continued this until one mission when it unsuccessfully tangled with the German Luftwaffe, and six of the twelve P-39s were lost. The 31st re-equipped with British Spitfire Mark Vs.

P-39s In The Mediterranean and Africa

Two squadrons of the 68th Observation Group, along with the 81st and 350th Fighter Groups, all from Twelfth Air Force, flew P-39D-1 and P-400 Airacobras in the Mediterranean Theatre which were diverted from Airacobras intended for the Soviet Union. These Airacobras were hampered by few spare parts and their mechanics were unfamiliar with servicing this fighter. This affected the pilot training given, and fewer Airacobras were deployed in North Africa by the end of 1942 than any other fighter type flown by the Twelfth Air Force. Many Airacobras were grounded in Portugal when ferried to their next combat zone because of this, and 18 were taken over by the Portugese Air Force. In July 1943, a Portugese Airacobra squadron was named the "Esquadrilla O.K.," or "O.K. Squadron." During May 1943, the Portugese air force sent two Colonels and a Major to Bell's factories in New York after confiscating the P-39s that had landed in their country. They had flown the Airacobras and were now interested in learning more about its production!

P-39s of the 350th Fighter Group escorted convoys and patrolled as part of the air defense of the coast of Africa. They were limited as their Airacobras could not intercept high flying enemy reconnaissance aircraft.

In January 1943, the Twelfth Air Support Command based in North Africa received additional P-39s for its 91st and 92nd Fighter Squadrons of the 81st Fighter Group. On January 22, ten P-39s of the 81st along with P-40s attacked and strafed trucks, tanks and machine gun nests in the Ousseltia Valley, the scene of heavy ground fighting with German forces. By January 26, the number of P-39s grew to 23. They were flown at low-levels for reconnaissance and strafing missions with Spitfires or P-40s flying overhead cover. The P-39s were extremely resistant to enemy flak damage (ground fire that exploded at predetermined altitudes). The enemy's push at Ousseltia was held, but by January 30, the German forces pressed again. By mid-morning, six P-39s, along with P-40s and A-20s, strafed the German tanks in Faid Pass that were attacking French forces. This raid destroyed a dozen tanks. All P-39s returned, but one was lost later that day on a strafing run. Most P-39s used in this operation were escorted by P-40s flying top cover. The 68th Observation Group's P-39s arrived in North Africa in late January 1943.

P-39s flying in the Tunisian (Africa) campaign

earned the nickname "Baby B-17s" because of the tremendous punishment they could take and return home. Any enemy target was fair game for the P-39 pilots in Africa. Bell Aircraft Corporation received pictures of P-39s returning with sand in their wing tips from brushing the soil on strafing passes, bullet holes in their propellers and controls shot out! Many Airacobra pilots felt comfortable flying under a hundred feet of altitude. Some preferred flying under telegraph wires rather than over!

By November 1943, the 350th Fighter Group moved to Sardinia, a major island southwest of Italy in the Mediterranean. It eventually moved north to Corsica and then into Italy. The 350th supported ground forces landing in Elba, an island between Corsica and northwest Italy, and later in France. The 350th merited a Distinguished Unit Citation for its activity on April 6, 1944, when its P-39s bombed and strafed enemy positions in western Italy. The 350th later transitioned into P-47s.

Bell test pilots flew P-39s with special 350-gallon droptanks to increase the Airacobra's range for Lend-Lease deliveries to Russia. To test this new configuration, Bell test pilot Jack Woolams, who was a college graduate and a former U.S. Army Air Corps pilot who came to Bell in July 1941 as a member of their Flight Research Staff, made a non-stop flight on October 2, 1942, from March Field, California, to Bolling Field, Washington, D.C. This 3,290 mile non-stop flight in a heavily fueled P-39 is thought to be the first non-stop cross-country trip in aviation history flown by an American fighter plane. It led to Airacobras flying to Russia instead of being shipped. When the war ended, several thousand P-39s were flown to Russia from the airport at Niagara Falls.

The P-39G

The P-39G, or Bell Model 26, followed in name only. On August 21, 1941, the Army Air Corps ordered 1,800 P-39G Airacobras, but the G was redesignated to later variants. No P-39Gs were ever assembled, as were no P-39H nor P-39I Airacobras. All orders were converted to later Airacobra variants.

The P-39J

The P-39J, or Bell Model 15B, was built in 25 examples under contract AC 15675 placed on September 13, 1940. These were serial numbers 41-7053 through 41-7056, and 41-7059 through 41-7079. The P-39J was nearly identical to the P-39F, but powered by an Allison V-1710-59 engine with automatic boost control.

The P-39K

The P-39K-1 was the first redesignated P-39G. It was nearly identical to the P-39D-2 except it was powered by a 1,325 horsepower V-1710-63 Allison engine turning an Aeroproducts propeller. A total of 210 were built using serial numbers 42-4244 through 42-4453. It had the same armament as the P-39D and similar performance, but it weighed 800 pounds more and had a slightly reduced flying range. Some P-39Ks were flown in New Guinea in 1943. The P-39K-2 designation was given to six P-39Ks modified for photo-reconnaissance.

The P-39L

The P-39L-1 followed, of which 250 were built using serial numbers 42-4454 through 42-4703. The P-39L added a streamlined low drag nosewheel. It could be fitted with wing rails to launch rockets in combat. The P-39L returned to the Curtiss Electric propeller. It had improved low-altitude performance. It was otherwise identical to the P-39D-2. P-39Ls flew in New Guinea and North Africa in 1943. P-39L-2s were eleven P-39Ls modified for photo-reconnaissance.

The P-39M

The P-39M arrived in November 1942 with a V-1710-67 Allison engine and an Aeroproducts propeller to improve its high-altitude performance, but only 10 more miles per hour were added at 15,500 feet. These Airacobras were used mostly for ground-attack. A total of 240 were assembled using serial numbers 42-4704 through 42-4943. A sub-variant, the P-39M-1, used the V-1710-83 Allison engine and a Curtiss Electric propeller. Its serial numbers were within those of the P-39M. Some P-39Ms flew in North Africa in 1944. Eight were modified for photo-reconnaissance and redesignated as the P-39M-2.

Bell test pilots visited Army Air Force bases during 1943 to deliver informal lectures to student pilots and discuss the P-39's flying characteristics. These pilots were well received after their visits were scheduled by

The P-39M also appeared as the P-39M-1, but each used a different propeller and Allison engine. This P-39M is 42-4756. BELL AIRCRAFT CORP. VIA TRUMAN A. PARTRIDGE, SR.

Bell's field representatives. One test pilot who participated was Jay Demming, who flew in the post-war Airacobra racing program. Gerald A. "Jay" Demming joined Bell Aircraft in September 1942. He became part of the Flight Research Staff after previously being a civilian pilot in the Royal Canadian Air Force. The visiting pilots boosted morale and promoted the Airacobra with P-39 pilots. Each visit usually included a P-39 demonstration flight which kept the visiting Airacobra test pilots in great demand at many Army Air Force training fields.

On January 1, 1943, Bell Aircraft Corporation began publishing an approximately twelve-page service bulletin for the P-39. The *Bell Serviceman* featured "Plane Pete," a cartoon character who presented many helpful hints for the proper servicing of the Airacobra. The "chief purpose of the *Bell Serviceman*," according to Volume 1, Issue 1, "is to serve as a clearing house for every useful bit of information you discover in the field, and for service tips developed here at the factory." The first issue reviewed, through narrative and Plane Pete's drawings, how to refuel the P-39's wing tanks, how to recover from a tailspin, what size wire to repair aileron trim tab hinges, how to clean supercharger vents and how to inspect gas tank floats affecting the gas gauges. Later issues covered similar topics and were presented in a light but serious manner which stressed servicing and flying the P-39 safely.

The May 5, 1943, issue of the *Bell Serviceman* stated that "if takeoff is delayed and coolant temperature rises above 125 degrees celsius . . . don't taxi back." Instead, the pilot was advised to "set the mixture control level to idle cut-off, and when the engine stops, turn the ignition off." Then "wait until the temperature goes down to a safe point. Don't overheat the engine! Be sure to watch that gauge!"

By July 15, 1943, the *Bell Serviceman* added a section called "Cobra Chatter," featuring short articles from the field about the P-39. The first "Cobra Chatter" noted Airacobra pilots in the southwest Pacific were dropping belly tanks containing a 50-50 mixture of engine oil and 100 octane gasoline along with incendiary sticks to ignite these improvised "bombs." It was referred to as a "deluxe Molotov cocktail" (a gasoline bomb). The newsletter further reported a Soviet Airacobra squadron had downed 142 different German and Italian fighters and bombers between June 1942 and March 1943.

The *Bell Serviceman* reported in its September 1, 1943 issue:

> The 37mm cannon carried by the Airacobra delivers, with each shot, 127,000 foot pounds of energy. Total for the five gun complement of the airplane, 179,000 foot pounds! This gives a gun horsepower of 1,395. With all guns firing, we obtain 47.5 strikes per second, having a total weight of 8.6 pounds, and hitting with a force equal to that of a five ton truck crashing into a wall at a speed of 33 miles per hour!. Now we know why bombers' wings rip off, Zeros burst into flame, subs grab their noses and head for deep water, and tanks grind their gears in anguish when the Cobras come a-calling!

In spring 1943, Bell Aircraft Corporation began publishing the "News from the Home Front to the Bell Service Representative," a several-page bulletin with data and stories relayed to Bell by its service representatives. These were typed and sent to every other field representative. This bulletin was published several times monthly to keep its personnel current on reports developed by Bell. Any changes in the P-39's service program were presented to inform its members about the latest changes with the Airacobra. Bell Aircraft's motto was, "The aircraft we build is not one iota better than the service that goes with it."

In May 1943, the most flying hours on a P-39 belonged to a P-39F, Army Air Force serial number 41-7223, with 1,124 hours and 35 minutes. Two weeks later, a P-39D-1, Army Air Force serial number 41-28267, was reported with 1,131 hours and 30 minutes! By the end of May, 41-28267 passed 1,172 hours while at Tonopah, Nevada. As the month closed, however, "old faithful," as Bell referred to 41-28267, with a total of 1,205 hours and 20 minutes, was lost in a mid-air collision.

By spring 1943, Bell Aircraft received information given by Japanese prisoners of war on Guadalcanal. They referred to the Airacobra as the "long-nosed bomber" "because of its deadly accuracy in laying those well-known 'eggs' just in the right spot at the right time." The Japanese referred to the P-39 as the "perpetual pest." "Two or more of those long-nosed bombers were always lurking over their sacred territory, ready at the least provocation to blow them to bits," according to Captain Ray Williams, the commander of the 68th Fighter Squadron on Guadalcanal.

The P-39N Becomes The First Large-Scale Airacobra Order

Despite the many Airacobra variants discussed thus far, the first large P-39 order came when Bell developed the P-39N-0 and P-39N-1 models, also known as the Bell Model 26. Bell constructed 2,095 P-39Ns using serial numbers 42-4944 through 42-5043, 42-8727 through 42-9726, 42-18246 through 42-18545, and 42-18546 through 42-19240. The P-39N used an Aeroproducts propeller and a different forward reduction gear. All P-39Ns, however, used the Allison V-1710-85 (E19) engine. Internal fuel capacity was reduced at the 167th P-39N from 120 U.S. gallons to 87 at the direction of the Army Air Force. This trimmed the maximum gross weight of the Airacobra by 350 pounds. Later P-39Ns used a curved armor plate to protect the pilot's head along with bulletproof glass in the cockpit. By April 1943, Bell received reports that the P-39N and P-39N-O were performing like interceptors. A Colonel Gillis from the Alaskan theatre advised Bell that "nothing will climb with the N-O. It is definitely an interceptor." A Commander Booth at Anacostia Naval Station, who had flown both the Airacobra and a captured Zero, noted the P-39 had the superior speed and rate of climb. Bell developed P-39N-3 and P-39N-5 sub-variants. Some P-39Ns were flown by the 18th Fighter Group on Guadalcanal from Henderson Field in June 1943. They were also flown by the Free French forces in North Africa during 1943 and by the Russians in the Soviet Union in 1944. In mid-May 1943, the last P-39N-5 Airacobra was assembled. Bell then produced P-39Qs.

During the darkest hours of early World War Two in spring 1940, France was overrun and occupied by the Germans. What was left of the French air force, the Armee de l'Air, escaped to England and formed the Free French air force. When the Allies freed Algiers in North Africa on the Mediterranean coastline in November 1942, French soil was freed as Algiers was controlled by France. The Free French air force moved its headquarters to Algiers. Free French air force flying units became operational in 1943 and participated with the British and Americans in attacks on Italy and Tunisia. The Free French helped liberate France and contribute to Germany's defeat. Two of their fighter groups flew P-39Ns in North Africa. They assembled their own P-39N-1 Airacobras with their own excellent assembly line techniques. One Free French test pilot commented the P-39N-1 was "the best plane he has flown." Before an interpreter was available, the Bell field representative

The first large-scale Airacobra order was the P-39N. This is a P-39N-0, 42-8926, seen in 1943.
BELL AIRCRAFT CORP. VIA TRUMAN A. PARTRIDGE, SR.

Larry Bell and Army Air Force acceptance test pilot Ritchie standing next to P-39K-1 42-4400 on October 26, 1942. A total of 210 "Ks" were built, but only one survives today. The significance of "Fireball" is not known.
BELL AIRCRAFT CORP. VIA TRUMAN A. PARTRIDGE, SR.

A P-39L, 42-4626, at Bell Aircraft Corporation. A total of 250 were built.
BELL AIRCRAFT CORP. VIA TRUMAN A. PARTRIDGE, SR.

The P-39M appeared during the winter of 1942-43. This one was test fitted with rocket rails. BELL AIRCRAFT CORP. VIA TRUMAN A. PARTRIDGE, SR.

The second "N" model was the P-39N-1. Despite sitting on snow-covered ramps at Buffalo, Airacobras flew in some of the world's hottest climates! BELL AIRCRAFT CORP. VIA TRUMAN A. PARTRIDGE, SR.

A Bell P-39N-5 at the factory. This test model had no nose cannon and all access panels were sealed off. BELL AIRCRAFT CORP. VIA TRUMAN A. PARTRIDGE, SR.

assisting in the assembly of the P-39s used sign language and any other means available to instruct in the assembly of the Airacobra! Bell later established a school in the field to train the French flying the P-39.

During World War Two, the Russian air force was designed and equipped to support the Russian army, and not to undertake its own separate strategic tasks. Rarely were the activities of the Russian air force separated from the daily activities of the army. It is easy to see why the P-39 was selected by the Russians as the Airacobra was designed for close ground-support, a mission it excelled at. P-39s equipped the 9th Guards Fighter Division and the 16th Guards Fighter Air Regiment of the Russian air force, two of the Soviets' best. Russian P-39s were put to their fullest use destroying German ground armor. By 1944, the Russian air force was in a position of air superiority over the Germans. The Red air force was massive, but tremendously efficient and capable.

Much has been written about the Airacobra's successful usage by the Russians. Some Russian pilots felt the P-39 outclassed even the German Bf-109. It is known that much of the fighting between Soviet P-39s and German Bf-109s was flown, however, below 10,000 feet where the P-39 was at its best. The Russians nicknamed the P-39 the "Cobrushka," or "little Cobra," as well as "Cobrastochka," or "dear little Cobra." Reports surfaced of German squadrons scattering when they met the "Stalin Falcons" in their P-39s. It is difficult to confirm the exploits of Russian P-39 fighter pilots, but several aces of the Soviet Union are known. The exploits of Lieutenant Colonel of the Guards Alexander I. Pokryshkin, a Russian squadron leader, are the most amazing. He was the Allies' leading ace of the war. He shot down 59 German aircraft with 48 of those in his own distinctly trimmed P-39. He was a Hero of the Soviet Union with at least three "Gold Star" medals from his country. He was one of nine pilots shooting down twenty or more enemy planes while flying P-39s. Pokryshkin was awarded the United States Distinguished Flying Cross by President Roosevelt. In September 1944, Lieutenant General L. C. Rudenko, Chairman of the Government Purchasing Commission for the Soviet Union, listed the other eight pilots' names with at least twenty P-39 kills. The four after Pokryshkin were Captain G. A. Rechkalov with 44 kills, then Captain N.

T. Guliav with 36, followed by the Klinka brothers; Major G. P. Klinka with 33, and Major B. B. Klinka with 26 victories. All were Heroes of the Soviet Union.

On May 28, 1943, Bell Aircraft Corporation premiered another publication, a weekly newspaper, the *Bell Aircraft News*. It was written for all company employees, with internal P-39 news and reports from the field. It also was stopped after the war, as was *The Bellringer.*

On July 19, 1943, Captain Charles Falletta, who flew P-39s in New Guinea and whose recovered P-39 in Australia is described later in this book's surviving aircraft section, spoke during a thirty minute Mutual network radio broadcast as part of the radio series, "The Army Air Forces." He reviewed his experiences with several Bell Aircraft workers.

In July 1943, Bell noted the first WASP (Womens Airforce Service Pilot) to fly the P-39 for Ferry Command was Mrs. Adele Scharr. She attended flying and familiarization training for the Airacobra at Bell's schools.

The Ultimate Airacobra, The P-39Q

Bell Aircraft did not produce a P-39O nor a P-39P. The next and final model was the P-39Q. It was assembled in the highest number of all Airacobra variants with 4,905 built. P-39Qs used serial numbers 42-19446 through 42-21250, 44-2001 through 44-4000, 44-32167 through 44-32666, and 44-70905 through 44-71504. More than half were transferred under Lend-Lease to the Soviet Union. Many Russian pilots preferred the P-39 over the P-40s supplied for ground-support duties. The P-39Q used an Allison V-1710-85 engine rated at 1,125 horsepower. It was faster than any other contemporary Russian fighter. It had a maximum speed of 376 miles per hour at 15,000 feet and an empty weight of 5,645 pounds. As a comparison with Russian fighters, the LA-5 had a maximum speed of 370 miles per hour. The LAGG-3 could fly at 279 miles per hour, the YAK-1 was capable of 335 miles per hour, the YAK-9 could fly 370 miles per hour, and the MiG-3 was capable of 360 miles per hour. All were piston-engine fighter planes. A total of 4,924 P-39s were sent to the Soviet Union of which 4,758 reached their locations. The P-39Q's height was increased to 12'5". Its service ceiling was 35,000 feet. It retained its 37mm nose cannon, its two .50 calibre nose machine guns with 200 rounds per gun and its ability to carry one bomb, but this final Airacobra model deleted its four .30 calibre wing machine guns. Instead it attached

The 17th P-39Q-1, 42-19462. The "Q" models are easily identified by their outboard .50-calibre machine gun pods under each wing. BELL AIRCRAFT CORP. VIA TRUMAN A. PARTRIDGE, SR.

The second P-39Q-5, 42-19597, at Bell with a long-range belly tank. This example survives today with the Confederate Air Force at San Marcos, Texas (see the survivors section). BELL AIRCRAFT CORP. VIA TRUMAN A. PARTRIDGE, SR.

The first P-39Q-10 Airacobras were delivered to the Army Air Force by the end of July 1943. This one, 42-21168, carries a long-range belly tank. BELL AIRCRAFT CORP. VIA TRUMAN A. PARTRIDGE, SR.

The first P-39Q-15 rolled off the assembly line on Aug. 29, 1943. This is the 506th Q-15, 44-2506. BELL AIRCRAFT CORP. VIA TRUMAN A. PARTRIDGE, SR.

This P-39Q-15, 44-2506, stands out against its snow-covered Buffalo surroundings. Photo taken during winter 1943-44. BELL AIRCRAFT CORP. VIA TRUMAN A. PARTRIDGE, SR.

Two Russia-bound Lend-Lease P-39Q-20 Airacobras waiting at Buffalo on Feb. 14, 1944. Note their long-range tanks and the lack of underwing .50-calibre machine gun pods. BELL AIRCRAFT CORP. VIA TRUMAN A. PARTRIDGE, SR.

The 474th P-39Q-20 high over Buffalo. Its tail number has been censored from this picture. BELL AIRCRAFT CORP. VIA TRUMAN A. PARTRIDGE, SR.

A P-39Q-20, 44-3572, stands before numerous other Airacobras bound for American and Russian bases. BELL AIRCRAFT CORP. VIA TRUMAN A. PARTRIDGE, SR.

a single faired-over .50 calibre machine gun under each outer wing panel armed with 300 rounds per gun. The weight of the protective armor varied among the various P-39Q production blocks. P-39Qs were produced briefly with four-bladed propellers before returning to the three-bladed versions for stability reasons. Some early P-39Qs carried 87 U.S. gallons internally, some carried 110, but most carried 120 U.S. gallons. By May 1943, the earliest P-39Qs were delivered to Eglin Field, Florida and Wright Field, Ohio for testing. By late June 1943, the P-39Q-5 was on the assembly line at Bell, but the P-39Q-10 was planned for production during the first week of July. By mid-July 1943, Bell added type A-1 bombsight adapters to 85 P-39Q-5 Airacobras at its Modification Center before delivering them.

The first P-39Q-10 Airacobras were delivered to the Army Air Force by the end of July 1943. This was Bell's highest monthly total for Airacobra deliveries. The Q-10 linked the throttle to the propeller setting to provide automatic adjustments. At the same time, Materiel Command advised Bell to eliminate manufacture, inspection and acceptance dates from P-39s and their components to prevent production information falling into enemy hands from wrecked or captured Airacobras.

The P-39Q-15 Airacobra was in production by the end of July 1943 and first rolled off Bell's assembly line on August 29, 1943. The Q-15 featured a reinforced inclined deck to prevent .50 calibre machine gun tripod mounting cracking, bulkhead reinforcements to prevent rudder pedal wall cracking, a reinforced reduction gearbox bulkhead to prevent cowling former cracking, and repositioning of the battery solenoid. Some P-39Q-20-BE Airacobras deleted the outer wing machine guns. P-39Q-21 and Q-25 Airacobras used four-bladed propellers. The P-39Q-30, however, was the last Airacobra model produced.

Another interesting note is that by the end of June 1943, Bell received field reports of P-39Qs successfully lifting 1,000-pound bomb loads within the United States. Some foreign air forces asked Bell for data on takeoff distances for P-39s equipped with even higher bomb loads! Some P-39Qs flew with the 318th Fighter Group at Oahu, Hawaii. They also flew in the South Pacific and Italy. First Lieutenant William A. Shomo, who later won the Medal of Honor flying the P-51, flew a P-39Q-5 with the 71st Tactical Reconnaissance Squadron in 1944 in New Guinea. His P-39Q was later recovered for display (see the survivors section elsewhere in this book).

By February 1944, the 332nd Fighter Group of the 15th Air Force in Italy was one of the last Army Air Force units to receive the Airacobra when 75 were delivered. These aircraft, however, were released two months later and replaced by P-47s. By April 1944, the 82nd and 110th Tactical Reconnaissance Squadrons turned in their Airacobras on New Guinea. P-39Qs were flown at training bases in the United States through the end of the war. P-39Qs were also flown by the Free French in North Africa, and the French air force flew their Airacobras until 1947. P-39Qs along with P-39Ns were flown by the Italians over the Balkans with the Co-Belligerent Air Force beginning in September 1944.

A year earlier, the Italian government under General Bagdolio had surrendered unconditionally to the Allies. On October 13, 1943, this government, which controlled those portions of Italy liberated by the Allies, declared war on Germany. The rest of Italy, however, was under German dominance. The next day, the free government was accepted as a Co-Belligerent. The United States Fifteenth Air Force turned over 75 P-39Qs from the 332nd Fighter Group and 74 P-39Ns to the Italians which were at a depot at Capodichino, Italy, near Naples. Many Italian pilots joined the newly formed Co-Belligerent Air Force on the eastern coast. The Fighter Wing consisted of five squadrons of which two, Squadrons 10 and 12, flew Bell P-39Q Airacobras with the others flying British Spitfires or Italian Macchi 202 and 205 fighters. These Co-Belligerent fighters, as well as their bombers and seaplanes, cooperated with the Balkan air force on 688 missions against German forces over Yugoslavia, which is east of Italy across the Adriatic Sea, by the end of the war in Europe (VE-Day).

The Italians flew their P-39s until 1950. They were among the last known Airacobras in military use. How long the Russians flew their P-39s in military service is not known. The last reported combat usage of the P-39 was by the North Korean Air Force in the early months of the Korean War during the summer of 1950. Their success was limited due to inexperienced pilots as well as having American F-51Ds and Lockheed F-80s as adversaries. The latter were easily 200 miles per hour faster!

The Two-Seat Trainer TP-39 Modification

One other variant of the P-39 should be noted. The TP-39 was a two-seat modification *kit* supplied by Bell Aircraft to field modify already produced P-39 models into trainers. It was not a separate factory model with its own separate serial numbers. In early July 1943, Bell reported the TP-39 in its *Home Front News* bulletin. Bell's Service Division received permission from the Army Air Force to modify one P-39 to a two-place trainer. The instructor sat in what was the gun compartment before with a new canopy extended forward to cover him or her. Some controls were provided for the instructor whereas the student pilot sat in the standard seat with full cockpit instruments. Bell referred to the modified Airacobra as a Tee Pee 39, which could be interpreted as either "two-place" or "trainer-pursuit." Some carried a wigwam or indian hut insignia and a "39." The trainer allowed new Airacobra pilots the opportunity to transition into a TP-39 before flying a standard single-seat P-39. The first TP-39 flew in August or September 1943. As pleasant looking as a typical P-39 was, the TP-39 modified Airacobra may be considered as one of the more unsightly aircraft of the Second World War!

Bell's training school, originally called Camp Cataract and later Camp Bell, closed on November 2, 1944 after graduating 7,432 P-39 and P-63 Kingcobra mechanics.

P-39 Production And Usage By 1944

By February 1944, the United States' inventory of Airacobras was at its peak with 2,105 P-39s. By August 1944, however, all first line fighter squadrons flying the P-39 had re-equipped with other later fighters from other manufacturers. The 347th Fighter Group was the last to fly the Airacobra in the Southwest Pacific in August 1944 before re-equipping with P-38s. On July 25, 1944, all P-39 production ceased at Bell Aircraft Corporation with 9,558 examples produced.

The first TP-39Q, 42-20024, actually modified from a P-39Q-5, as seen on Sept. 16, 1943. The teepee insignia is seen below the canopy. BELL AIRCRAFT CORP. VIA TRUMAN A. PARTRIDGE, SR.

Interesting picture of a Lend-Lease P-39Q-25. The melting snow reflects the presence of several other Russia-bound Airacobras. Photo taken March 14, 1944. BELL AIRCRAFT CORP. VIA TRUMAN A. PARTRIDGE, SR.

Lend-Lease P-39Q-25 Airacobras with four-bladed propellers, not often seen on production P-39s. The B-25 in the foreground was most likely also a Lend-Lease transfer. BELL AIRCRAFT CORP. VIA TRUMAN A. PARTRIDGE, SR.

The last Airacobras on the assembly line at Bell. Serial number 44-71422 was within the last 100 P-39Qs built. Photo taken spring 1944. BELL AIRCRAFT CORP. VIA TRUMAN A. PARTRIDGE, SR.

The final P-39! Serial number 44-71504 precedes a line of P-63s, its younger sibling. Photo taken July 1, 1944. BELL AIRCRAFT CORP. VIA TRUMAN A. PARTRIDGE, SR.

Airacobra production ceased at 9,558 P-39s assembled on July 25, 1944, when the last P-39Q-30, 44-71504, was completed. BELL AIRCRAFT CORP. VIA TRUMAN A. PARTRIDGE, SR.

Bell test pilot Jay Demming prepares 44-71504 for its final acceptance flight on Aug. 5, 1944. His crew chief was Tony Celaro. Demming later flew *Cobra II* in the 1947 Thompson Trophy Race. BELL AIRCRAFT CORP. VIA TRUMAN A. PARTRIDGE, SR.

P-39 Derivatives Before And During The War

As with many other highly produced fighter aircraft designs from Second World War, the P-39 had several derivatives. Some were more successful than others. They were:

■ *XFL-1 Airabonita.* In 1938, the United States Navy held a design competition to develop a new high-performance carrier fighter. On November 8, 1938, they ordered an experimental aircraft carrier version of the P-39 under contract number 63629, despite Bell having no prior experience building aircraft carrier planes. This fighter was called the XFL-1 Airabonita. Competing with the XFL-1 was Vought's XF4U-1 Corsair and Grumman's twin-engine XF5F-1 Skyrocket. The Airabonita had a pair of main landing gears located closer to the leading edge of its wing but no tricycle gear as in the Airacobra. The XFL-1 was a tail-dragger design with an arrestor hook and catapult spools located in its tail section as required for aircraft carrier landings. It also had underwing radiators which the P-39 did not have. Only one was assembled with Bureau Number 1588.

The Airabonita flew on May 13, 1940. It was painted overall Navy grey except for the upper wing surfaces which were chrome yellow. The Airabonita had a longer wingspan but a shorter fuselage than the Airacobra. It had a taller canopy as its pilot sat higher in the cockpit. The plane was strengthened for the more rigorous carrier landings. The XFL-1 was powered by an Allison XV-1710-6 engine rated at 1,150 horsepower driving a Curtiss three-bladed propeller. The prototype was not armed although production models would have been.

The Navy began flight testing the XFL-1 in July 1940 at Naval Air Station Anacostia, Virginia, after a six-month delay due to wing dihedral redesign and ballasting problems, but engine and balance problems delayed the testing until April 7 to April 29, 1941.

The Airabonita failed its carrier qualifying trials due to landing gear problems and a difficulty with the tail rising during carrier landings. On May 12, 1914, the Navy stated, "The XFL-1 is found to be unsatisfactory for use as a carrier fighter or for arrested landings." It was returned to Bell in December 1941 for changes. It resumed flight testing at the Navy's newly opened Patuxent River Test Center in Maryland in early 1942 by which time the XFL-1's production was cancelled.

By then, the Corsair was deemed the most successful design. The Airabonita was underpowered with a top speed of 336 miles per hour at 11,000 feet, well below a standard P-39's performance despite having both a supercharger and a turbo-supercharger. The Airabonita remained at the Patuxent station but any reuseable parts were removed. Its demise came when it was dumped. The remains of the Airabonita sit inverted today on the banks of the Patuxent River at or near the Navy's test center where its deteriorated wreckage is sadly used as landfill material.

The XFL-1 was Bell's attempt to build an aircraft carrier version of the P-39 for the Navy. Only one Airabonita was completed. BELL AIRCRAFT CORPORATION

■ *A-7.* A proposed radio-controlled version of the P-39 that did not go into development.

■ *F2L-1K.* In June 1945, the United States Navy acquired two P-39s, RP-39Q-5-BE, Army Air Force serial number 42-19976, and RP-39Q-10-BE, Army Air Force serial number 42-20807, for conversion to radio-controlled target drones. These aircraft were assigned new Bureau Numbers 91103 and 91102. A conversion contract was awarded to Bell, contract number NOAS-7317, to modify these two P-39Qs. These Airacobras, at first called F2L-1Ks and later XTDL-1s, were the first target drones with all electric controls. This provided improved handling during evasive maneuvers. The F2L-1Ks also carried auto-pilots. They were capable of 350 miles per hour up to 25,000 feet with just over three hours flight endurance. Bell delivered 91103 and 91102 to the Cape May Naval Station in New Jersey on February 10, 1946, for acceptance by the Navy to begin flight testing the following week. On April 3, 1946, 91102 suffered engine failure and made a wheels up landing incurring serious damage. It was stripped of useable parts and struck off charge. The remaining F2L-1K was moved to the Chincoteague Naval Air Station in Virginia to resume testing. On July 11, 1946, 91103 was also severely damaged when its left main gear brakes locked. It was also struck off charge, effectively bringing the Navy's Airacobra target drone program to a halt. Five more P-39s were to be delivered to the Navy for conversion, but the program was cancelled and the transfer not completed.

■ *P-63.* The P-63 was the P-39's most successful descendant. The Kingcobra, as it was named, was similar to the P-39 in appearance but was a totally new fighter plane. There were no interchangeable structural parts between the P-39 and the P-63. The three XP-39Es described earlier served as test beds for the P-63. A total of 3,303 Kingcobras were assembled, but none flew combat with the United States Army Air Force as the North American P-51 Mustang was fulfilling that role. Most P-63s went overseas to the air forces of other countries, generally the Russians and the Free French. The P-63 had larger external dimensions than the P-39. It had a redesigned laminar flow wing. It used a two-stage engine-driven supercharger, something the production P-39s badly needed, and the P-63 had better access to its armament despite having the same armament as the P-39Q. P-63s used four-bladed propellers instead of the three-bladed units on the P-39. The prototype XP-63 flew on December 7, 1942.

The P-39's successor, the P-63 Kingcobra. BELL AIRCRAFT CORPORATION

■ *L-39.* The L-39, of which two were assembled, was actually the first swept-wing American research fighter plane. The L-39s were based on two converted P-63s, and *not* on the P-39. Bell undertook this testing program at the request of the Navy after the war. During the L-39 program, Bell re-purchased two P-39s in addition to the two converted P-63s. Bell needed to buy the P-39s' lighter propellers for the L-39 program because of the L-39s' center of gravity balancing problems encountered during testing, and it was cheaper to buy used P-39s as a whole. Two P-39Qs were repurchased from the War Assets Administration for $750 each, whereas new propellers alone cost $1,500! Later at Bell, these two P-39Qs—less their propellers—were pulled from storage and became the famous racing *Cobra I* and *Cobra II* which were refitted with the propellers not needed on the L-39s, the former four-bladed P-63 propellers. A.M. "Tex" Johnston and Chalmers H. "Slick" Goodlin were two of Bell's test pilots who flew the L-39s. They were involved in the racing P-39 program after the war. Tests conducted with the L-39s led to improvements in the low speed handling characteristics of the swept wing, a serious problem with many early swept wing designs. The L-39 test program was cancelled in August 1946. The L-39s were sold for scrap by NACA at the Ravenna Arsenal in February 1955.

The L-39 was a swept-wing P-63 and not a P-39 at all.
BELL AIRCRAFT CORPORATION

Bell Aircraft Production In New York Summarized

In a statement given on October 10, 1945 before the Sub-Committee on Aircraft and Light Metals of the Special Committee Investigating the National Defense Program of the United States Senate, Larry Bell related the following facts: In 1940, Bell Aircraft produced 220,000 pounds of airframes. During 1944, the company produced 30,346,000 pounds of airframes, an increase factor of 138 times more production in five years. Employment went from around 1,200 employees in 1940 to over 50,000 at Bell's peak in February 1944, an increase factor of 42 times more people employed. The Buffalo and Niagara divisions in New York produced over 12,900 fighter planes including Airacudas, Airacobras, Kingcobras and Airacomets, with enough spare parts to raise this total to an equivalent of over 16,000 airplanes built for World War Two. About 60 percent of Bell's fighter aircraft were sent to Russia under Lend-Lease. Both New York divisions had sales in excess of $600 million.

P-39s After World War Two

As with the P-51, the Corsair and other World War Two fighter aircraft, there was life after the Second World War for the P-39. All military Airacobras were retired from service worldwide within a few years. The Army Air Force in the United States disposed of all Army Air Force P-39s during 1946, with most being scrapped after useable contents were removed. Surviving P-39s were most often seen in air racing in the United States during the late 1940s, and some with great success.

When the war ended, the public's interest in air racing was revived. Instead of contestants arriving at the national air races with homemade designs, however, they brought modified World War Two fighter planes which the government had spent huge sums of money researching and developing in the decade before 1946. Better yet, there was an abundance of high-performance, low air time and newly obsoleted propeller driven fighter planes, which the War Assets Administration was eager to sell to the public for as little as $600 to $1,000, ready to fly, which was a fraction of their original cost. This philosophy held true for ex-military P-39s as much as for P-51s or Corsairs. Once purchased, by reducing the unnecessary weight of armor and armament, adding a later model engine than the one in the plane when assembled, along with a few aerodynamic modifications and a polished paint scheme, most former World War Two fighter planes made excellent pylon or closed course contenders.

The P-39 was a good candidate for air racing. The engine in the middle of the fuselage established the plane's mass in its center section, which made the P-39 very light on the controls. It was also a very clean design. The P-63, its successor, possessed a more advanced supercharged Allison engine. It was relatively easy to transplant a P-63's improved engine into a much lighter P-39 and build a good racer. It became a hybrid airplane utilizing the best of both designs to their fullest combined advantage. Later model P-63s used Allison engines with two-stage supercharging wherein one supercharger forced its output into the second supercharger. Combined with special racing fuels, some tremendous manifold pressures could be achieved at low altitudes for air racing. These later Allison engine designs were far superior to the standard E series engines originally powering the P-39s. Finally, an improved propeller from a P-63 increased a modified P-39's performance and used the extra power to its best advantage.

There were several P-39s modified for air racing such as NX57591, a P-39Q now displayed at the National Air and Space Museum and described in the survivors section, and N13381, a P-39L owned by James Harp, Bendix Race Number 95, that was first flown in a bare metal finish and later painted yellow with black trim that used a four-bladed propeller. It was flown in the 1949 Sohio Trophy Race and finished ninth. But perhaps the most famous racing P-39s after the war were a pair of P-39Q racers, NX92847 and NX92848, better known as *Cobra I* and *Cobra II.*

The Legendary Cobra I and Cobra II

A. M. "Tex" Johnston and Jack Woolams were both Bell Aircraft test pilots associated with the X-1 sound barrier rocket-powered planes. "Tex" Johnston joined their Flight Research staff in March 1943. Prior to coming to Bell, he had been an instructor for two years with the Army Air Corps as well as a pilot with Ferry Command for six months. He had been a licensed pilot since age 18. He had 2,300 hours flying time including multi-engine experience when he joined Bell. Tex Johnston and Jack Woolams decided that P-39s equipped with more powerful P-63 Allison engines and freed of their military hardware would be contenders at the Thompson Trophy Race held in 1946 in Cleveland. Many ex-military fighter planes would be in contention, and these gentlemen felt that specially prepared P-39s would be in the running for the prestigious trophy. Their idea was presented to Bell's president, Larry Bell. He said he would extend Bell Aircraft's expertise and shop facilities to them, but the project would not have direct sponsorship by Bell Aircraft. Woolams and Johnston joined forces with a third Bell test pilot, "Slick" Goodlin, who was also associated with the X-1 test program, under the named sponsorship of Goodlin's own private company, Skylanes Unlimited. Woolams and Johnston located the two stored P-39Q-10-BE Airacobras at Bell Aircraft that were bought back from the military to obtain their three-bladed propellers for the unrelated L-39 test program. Skylanes Unlimited purchased the unneeded P-39s less their propellers from Bell for the sum of $1 each!

Skylanes assumed operation at Niagara Falls Municipal Airport. Approximately a dozen Bell mechanics and engineers went on leave of absence to work for Skylanes to prepare the two racing P-39s. Woolams and Johnston would fly the modified Airacobras and Goodlin would be the spare pilot. Both P-39s underwent only moderate modifications. All military hardware was removed. Bladder cell fuel tanks replaced the self-sealing units. The landing gears were improved to retract in five seconds for faster takeoffs. The Pitot

Jack Woolams with his unpainted *Cobra I* on Aug. 20, 1946. The P-63 propeller and the pitot tube within the spinner are both seen. BELL AIRCRAFT CORP. VIA TRUMAN A. PARTRIDGE, SR.

Tex Johnston with his unpainted *Cobra II*. The twelve exhaust stacks on each side of the V-1710-135 (G4) Allison engine can be seen behind the cockpit door. BELL AIRCRAFT CORP. VIA TRUMAN A. PARTRIDGE, SR.

Tex Johnston, Slick Goodlin and Jack Woolams in front of the 1946 Thompson Trophy winner, *Cobra II*, before it was painted. Photo taken on Aug. 20, 1946. BELL AIRCRAFT CORP. VIA TRUMAN A. PARTRIDGE, SR.

tube, which tells the airspeed indicator and thus the pilot how fast the plane is travelling, was relocated to the nose section projecting through the center of the propeller shaft where the cannon had been. These racing P-39s were now over a thousand pounds lighter.

Nowhere was change more apparent in these modified Airacobras than in their engine compartments. Skylanes obtained four much more powerful Allison V-1710-135 (G4) engines with twelve exhaust stacks per side from government surplus. This model was used in the improved Bell P-63F Kingcobra late in the war. The engines were rebuilt with domed pistons and a water/alcohol injection system to allow the P-39s to race at much faster speeds. With the faster engines, the installation of four-bladed P-63 propellers, which were exchanged from the Navy's L-39s, proved ideal. Some problems were noted in the follow up test program, but these were generally resolved. The control surfaces, which were previously fabric covered, were now reskinned in a metal covering to prevent control surface fluttering and instability at higher speeds. When completed, the P-39Qs were faster than 420 miles per hour at low level flight. They were next christened *Cobra I* and *Cobra II*, with *I* being painted bright red, and *II* painted chrome yellow. Both received identical black-spiked trim to their noses, sides and tail surfaces contrasting their base colors.

The Thompson Trophy Race, also known as the National Air Races, was sponsored by the Thompson Products Company. The race was first flown in 1930, and it ran until 1939 when it stopped due to the war. It resumed again after the war. The 1946 race was a five day event held over Labor Day weekend at the Cleveland, Ohio, airport. It had several corporate sponsors, among them Kendall Oil, Sohio, and Allison Motors, the manufacturer of the engines used in the P-39, the P-63 and many other World War Two aircraft. The race course's length was increased from ten miles used before the war to thirty miles. The route flown was essentially square shaped, averaging seven and a half miles on the four legs. A "racehorse start" was used from the pre-war era. In the entire post-war history of the Thompson Trophy Race, *Cobra II* was the only P-39 to both qualify and compete in the race.

On August 27, 1946, both Skylanes Unlimited

modified P-39s flew west to Cleveland. On the 29th, both pilots qualified their Airacobras for the Thompson Trophy Race, with Jack Woolams placing the red *Cobra I* at 392.7 miles per hour, and Tex Johnston turning in an incredible 409.1 miles per hour in the yellow *Cobra II*. Woolams, however, returned *Cobra I* to Niagara Falls to replace its Allison engine with one of the other modified spares. By late August 30th, the second engine was securely in place. Woolams flew out over Lake Ontario in *Cobra I*. At about 6:30 p.m., *Cobra I* rolled to its left side and crashed into Lake Ontario. Woolams' body was recovered on the 31st, but *Cobra I* never was. Based on eyewitness accounts, Bell Aircraft engineers concluded the Airacobra's speed in excess of 400 miles per hour plus the torque-generated twisting forces developed by the powerful engine and four-bladed P-63 propeller had caused the Plexiglas canopy to implode onto Woolams. *Cobra II*, the other racing Airacobra, underwent further modifications. A safety wire was added to *Cobra II*'s windshield, and four one-quarter inch thick strips of aluminum were attached to strengthen the rear fuselage. Larry Bell had intended for Jack Woolams to be the first man to break the speed of sound in the X-1, and his death profoundly affected Mr. Bell.

On Monday, September 3, 1946, *Cobra II* was ready for the final race of the 1946 Thompson Trophy races. There were five P-51D Mustangs in contention with one Corsair, one P-38 Lightning and four P-63s, the P-39's successor. It was a very impressive roster.

When the race started at about 4 p.m., Tex Johnston in *Cobra II* with race number 84 roared down the runway and got off the ground with *Cobra II*'s wheels tucked away faster than anyone on the field. At the end of three laps, the bright yellow Airacobra was far in the lead, so Tex Johnston eased back on the throttle. He held the lead to the finish, completing the race in 48 minutes and 8 seconds. He averaged 373 miles per hour on the Thompson's 300 mile long race course. Tex Johnston received both the Thompson Trophy and the Allegheny-Ludlum Trophy for his new closed course speed record. *Cobra II* returned to Niagara Falls unbeaten, but Bell Aircraft soon denied some of its pilots future pylon racing. Tex Johnston returned to his flying at Bell as the chief test pilot as he was occupied with the X-1 rocket plane test program. *Cobra II* seemed in forced retirement despite an impressive victory.

Cobra II, however, did not stay idle long. The next racing season saw another Bell test pilot, Jay Demming, convince an Indianapolis car dealer, Rollin Stewart, to buy *Cobra II* for $10,000. It was quickly prepared for the 1947 Thompson race.

Tex Johnston, Slick Goodlin and Jack Woolams on Aug. 20, 1946. *Cobra II* is on the left and *Cobra I* is on the right.
BELL AIRCRAFT CORP. VIA TRUMAN A. PARTRIDGE, SR.

Cobra I with Jack Woolams at the controls on Aug. 26, 1946. This picture was taken the day before Woolams and Johnston flew to Cleveland for the 1946 Thompson Trophy Race. *Cobra I* crashed into Lake Ontario on Aug. 30, killing Woolams.
BELL AIRCRAFT CORP. VIA TRUMAN A. PARTRIDGE, SR.

Tex Johnston and *Cobra II* on Aug. 26, 1946.
BELL AIRCRAFT CORP. VIA TRUMAN A. PARTRIDGE, SR.

Cobra II nearly perished in the same manner as *Cobra I*. On the final qualifying lap before the Thompson race, *Cobra II*'s left cockpit door imploded, but Jay Demming landed safely. Standard P-39 doors were fitted to *Cobra II* as a result.

When the 1947 Thompson began, twelve other ex-military race-prepared surplus World War Two fighters took to the air with *Cobra II*. Four of the thirteen racers crashed, and one pilot was killed. Two Corsairs in the group placed first and second, and *Cobra II* with Jay Demming aboard placed third at an average speed of 389.8 miles per hour, faster than in 1946, but less than the 396.1 needed to win in 1947.

In 1948, Rollin Stewart sold *Cobra II* to his attorney and forced Jay Demming out. A new pilot, Charles F. Brown, the chief test pilot with Allison engines, was selected. A three-bladed propeller was added to make *Cobra II* more stable. Brown and Allison engineer Don Nolan used a loaned prototype G6 Allison engine that was not otherwise available for racing. This radical new engine had two-stage supercharging and a Bendix fuel injection system. It was added to the yellow Airacobra. The Pitot tube was moved back onto the wing. The P-39 was now renamed the KF-1 instead of *Cobra II*, as Kaiser-Frazer, a now defunct automobile manufacturer, also sponsored the air racer. The words KAISER FRAZER appeared above and below the exhaust stacks on the plane's fuselage sides.

For the 1948 Thompson race, Brown qualified at an incredible 418 miles per hour and received the number one pole position. As the race began, the rapid acceleration of the Airacobra again took command as it had in 1946, and the KF-1 was the first to climb the skies. A tight race soon followed. Brown decided to keep

Tex Johnston departs Niagara Falls for Cleveland and the Thompson Trophy Race on Aug. 27, 1946.
BELL AIRCRAFT CORP. VIA TRUMAN A. PARTRIDGE, SR.

The 1946 Thompson Trophy winner, *Cobra II*, piloted to first place by Tex Johnston.
BELL AIRCRAFT CORP. VIA TRUMAN A. PARTRIDGE, SR.

the KF-1's engine turning at full power to set a new speed record. One lap was completed at 413 miles per hour. But on the 19th of the 20 laps in total, the big modified Allison engine expired, and the bright yellow leading racer landed after averaging 392 miles per hour. A P-51D later won at 384 miles per hour, but only this Mustang and two other racers from the ten starting aircraft finished the race. The problem causing the Airacobra's engine to quit was a loose section of the engine cowling that exposed the rear engine to exhaust stack heat. This overheated the fuel line causing a vapor lock, and the engine quit from fuel starvation. The KF-1 was ferried back to Indianapolis, but ran out of fuel a mile short of the airport and was damaged on landing. Owner Stewart did not repair it for the 1949 Thompson. The P-39 sat for years in a hangar in Indianapolis.

Cobra II Color Schemes

1946: Overall yellow with black rudder, spinner, Pitot tube in nose and spikes reversing back from the nose. Race number 84 on aft fuselage, NX92848 vertically on the fin, "P-39 Airacobra built by Bell Aircraft" on the doors, *Cobra II* on the forward fuselage along with names Tex Johnston and Skylanes Unlimited. Four-bladed propeller.

1947: To the engine exhaust panel was added KAISER FRAZER above and below, *Cobra II* still on nose, but the doors said "Jay Demming" with two decals below his name. Below the doors it said "Stewart Motor Sales, Inc., Indianapolis, Ind." The aft fuselage now had race number 11. Black on spinner, spikes, rudder and Pitot tube. Four-bladed propeller.

1948: The rear Plexiglas behind the pilot was faired over and painted yellow with a Kendall decal. Still race #11. Below the air intake on the aft fuselage it said "Revere." The rudder now had a checkerboard pattern on it. Still said KAISER FRAZER on side. Chuck Brown was on the doors along with EXPERIMENTAL, but no decals. It still said "Stewart Motor Sales, Inc. Indianapolis, Ind." below the doors. A small star was painted on the forward fuselage below the windshield. *Cobra II* was gone, and "KF-1" replaced it. No more black spikes on the nose. Three-bladed propeller.

Cobra II, or KF-1, did not race in 1949. After that, the air races were halted because of the Korean War. Ed Maloney bought the Airacobra in 1960 when it was located in derelict condition. He restored it to a wartime military paint scheme and displayed it for many years in his Air Museum in Claremont, California. It was damaged in a landing accident when its wheels failed to extend.

In 1967, Mike Carroll, who had raced a Hawker Sea Fury before, bought Ed Maloney's Airacobra. He planned to break the world piston-engine speed record in the once famous P-39. To do this, a highly modified V-1710-CG Allison engine was added at Pylon Air in Long Beach, California which developed 2,850 horsepower. A four-bladed propeller was added. The left door and lower radiator were removed. All seams were filled and sanded. To further attempt breaking the 500 miles per hour limit, four feet of outer wing was removed from each tip. In conjunction with the instability effects that four-bladed propellers had had in the past on this and other Airacobras, this was a very surprising modification.

Mike Carroll began taxiing tests during the summer of 1968. On August 10, 1968, he took off for his modified Airacobra's first test flight. As he climbed to 2,000 feet, the P-39 yawed to the left, snaprolled to the right, and then began spinning towards the ground. Carroll bailed out through the cockpit door, but apparently his body hit the tail section, and he never pulled his parachute's ripcord. *Cobra II* was destroyed in the crash.

Thus ended the career of the surviving semi-factory sponsored Airacobra, NX92848, once known as *Cobra II*. It and its red-trimmed sibling were surely the two most famous and colorful Airacobra race planes.

Conclusion

Today, over a half century after the P-39 was designed, the Airacobra must still bear the scorn heaped upon it during its active service life. It has been criticized for its "low (service) ceiling, slow rate of climb and relative lack of maneuverability." Its ten-foot extension shaft between the engine and the propeller was criticized for fatiguing its pilots. Sometimes P-39s were blamed for spinning or tumbling for no apparent reason when trimmed incorrectly. Some accounts stated the P-39 was "practically useless over 17,000 feet."

Yet in the final analysis, the P-39 was a pursuit fighter that was either born too early, or asked to stay on the front line and fight too long to perform a mission for which it simply was not designed. Its future was planned from a poor military perspective between 1937 to 1940, and its airframe was redesigned and reduced to meet those inferior pre-war plans. It was a ground-attack fighter asked to perform a dual role, but stripped of the means for accomplishing that additional role. Without its turbo-supercharger, the production P-39 was moderately inferior to some other Axis enemy fighter planes. Had it been properly equipped with a turbo-supercharger, or later equipped with a Rolls Royce Merlin engine such as the P-51 Mustang was allowed to transition into during its service life, then the P-39 may possibly be remembered today with the same admiration as the P-51.

As it was, it was the most underrated American fighter plane of World War Two. It compared favorably or excelled in many respects with its closest ally of the same vintage, the P-40. The P-39 was a well-built, reliable airplane capable of handling an incredible amount of aerial damage. Its ten-foot extension shaft has been credited with almost doubling the life of its Allison engine. It excelled at low-level ground-support, and it maintained tremendous firepower. It also possessed excellent flying characteristics. Most importantly, the P-39 was available in good numbers, along with the P-40, in the dark, early days of World War Two, long before adequate numbers of P-38s, P-47s and P-51s were available. By the end of the war, more P-39s (9,558) were built than P-38 Lightnings (9,535). The P-39 was there when America needed it the most, and it did the job it was designed for. It is a shame that only 35 P-39s survive today.

America owes the Airacobra the same gratitude as is now paid to the P-40, the P-38, the P-47 and the P-51. The P-39 was America's first modern fighter aircraft design in World War Two. The Airacobra should never be forgotten for the major role it played in our early military effort in World War Two. It deserves better.

The P-39 forward fuselage assembly before the cabin was attached. This rigid one-piece unit later held the engine, driveshaft and propeller reduction gears. BELL AIRCRAFT CORP. VIA TRUMAN A. PARTRIDGE, SR.

ABOVE: Completing the cockpit and the forward fuselage.
BELL AIRCRAFT CORP. VIA TRUMAN A. PARTRIDGE, SR.

LEFT: The nose section contained the cannon, two machine guns, reduction gearbox, nosegear and armor plating.
BELL AIRCRAFT CORP. VIA TRUMAN A. PARTRIDGE, SR.

ABOVE: Final assembly on a line of P-39s.
BELL AIRCRAFT CORP. VIA TRUMAN A. PARTRIDGE, SR.

RIGHT: Installing the nosewheel and strut assembly.
BELL AIRCRAFT CORP. VIA TRUMAN A. PARTRIDGE, SR.

COMPARISON SECTION

A comparison of the P-39 with several contemporary fighter aircraft of the Second World War.

1935

7-35	Bell Aircraft Corporation is formed.
9-35	The prototype German Messerschmitt Bf-109 flies. (The Bf-109 will eventually be manufactured in higher numbers than any other warplane of World War Two.)

1936

6-36	Bell begins designing its Model 4 (the P-39).
12-36	Prototype Bf-109s are sent to Spain to fly under combat conditions in the Spanish Civil War.

1937

Early '37	The production Bf-109B is issued to an operational German fighter unit. Its maximum speed is 292 miles per hour.
3-19-37	The American Army Air Corps invites American aircraft companies to design a new pursuit airplane.
Spring '37	The first Lockheed P-38 Lightning drawings begin.
5-18-37	Bell submits its Model 4 proposal to the Army Air Corps.
6-37	The prototype XP-38 is ordered.
7-37	The prototype Curtiss XP-40 Warhawk is ordered. It is a reworked P-36A.
10-7-37	The Army Air Corps orders one Bell Model 4 and redesignates it the XP-39.
11-11-37	The Bf-109D sets a speed record at 379 miles per hour.

1938

3-38	Bell unveils the XP-39 at its Buffalo plant.
1938	Twelve Bf-109Cs are sent to Spain for combat.
10-38	The prototype XP-40 flies. Its maximum speed is 342 miles per hour.

1939

1939	Republic begins work on its AP-10 fighter (the P-47 Thunderbolt's predecessor).
1-27-39	The prototype XP-38 flies.
Spring '39	The first production Bf-109Es reach German Luftwaffe units. Their maximum speed is 354 miles per hour. They will be Germany's primary fighter in the Battle of Britain during the summer and autumn of 1940.
4-1-39	The prototype Japanese A6M1 Zero fighter flies.
4-6-39	The XP-39 flies. Its maximum speed is 390 miles per hour.
4-39	Thirteen pre-production YP-39s are ordered by the Army Air Corps.
4-26-39	The prototype Zero attains 304 miles per hour.
4-27-39	The Army Air Corps orders 524 P-40s. Thirteen pre-production YP-38s are also ordered.
8-1-39	Republic offers its AP-10 fighter to the Army Air Corps. It is rejected, but an enlarged version is requested instead.
8-10-39	The Army Air Corps orders 80 P-39Cs and 66 more YP-38s.
9-39	The Bf-109E becomes the Luftwaffe's standard fighter.
11-39	The prototype XP-47 is ordered by the Army Air Corps along with a stripped XP-47A.
11-25-39	The XP-39 is called the XP-39B. It resumes flight tests, but achieves 375 miles per hour.
12-39	Zero production begins in Japan.

1940

4-13-40	The Royal Air Force orders 675 Model 14 export Airacobras.
4-40	North American Aviation offers to design a new fighter to answer the British Air Purchasing Commission's request to build Hawk 87A-1s (P-40s) for the British. (This new plane will become the P-51, perhaps the best high-altitude escort fighter of World War Two.)

5-40	The first production P-40s appear. Maximum speed is 357 miles per hour. The British order 560 P-40Ds.
6-5-40	The British order 667 P-38s, but without turbo-superchargers.
8-40	The first Japanese Zeros appear over Chungking, China.
9-4-40	The Army Air Corps cancels the XP-47 and XP-47A. They instead order the revised XP-47B.
9-13-40	The YP-39s fly and achieve 368 miles per hour.
9-16-40	The YP-38 flies and achieves 405 miles per hour.
9-20-40	The North American NA-73 is redesignated the XP-51.
9-40	The Army Air Corps orders the P-40D. Its maximum speed is 352 miles per hour. They also order 171 P-47Bs, 602 P-47Cs, and 607 additional P-38s.
10-26-40	The prototype NA-73X (P-51) flies. Britain orders 320 examples.

1941

1-41	Upgraded Bf-109Fs reach operational Luftwaffe units. They outperform their primary opponent, the British Spitfire, at higher altitudes. Their maximum speed is 390 miles per hour. The first P-39C flies, and 17 are delivered to the Army Air Corps.
2-41	The first P-39Ds enter the Army Air Corps. They are the first combat-ready Airacobras.
4-10-41	Two P-39Ds are modified into XP-39Es. They later reach a maximum speed of 386 miles per hour.
5-1-41	The first production P-51 flies.
5-6-41	The prototype XP-47B flies. (It became history's largest and heaviest single-seat piston-engine fighter.)
5-22-41	The P-40D flies.
7-3-41	The first export Model 14 Airacobras arrive in England. They achieve 367 miles per hour.
8-41	P-38Ds reach the Army Air Corps. They are the first combat-ready Lightnings.
8-21-41	1,800 P-39Gs are ordered but are delivered as later model Airacobras.
10-9-41	The Royal Air Force flies its only Airacobra mission over France.
12-7-41	The Japanese attack Pearl Harbor and draw the United States into World War Two the next day. More than 400 Zeros have been delivered. Their maximum speed is 338 miles per hour.
12-10-41	The American Volunteer Group in China under General Chennault draws its first blood against the Japanese while flying P-40s.
12-41	The Royal Air Force withdraws the Airacobra, but the Army Air Corps sends the P-39 into action in Alaska, Australia and the Panama Canal Zone.

1942

1942	The P-40F begins production.
3-42	P-38Es reach the Army Air Corps. Production P-47Bs leave the assembly line. Their maximum speed is 429 miles per hour.
4-6-42	P-39s score their first hits on Japanese aircraft.
4-42	P-51s enter British service. Non-turbo-supercharged P-38s are tested by the British. Their performance is so poor that the Lightnings are rejected and returned.
5-42	Army Air Corps P-39s serve in the Aleutians.
6-42	P-47Bs enter the Army Air Corps. The P-38G appears with a maximum speed of 400 miles per hour.
Summer '42	Army Air Corps P-39s fly against the Luftwaffe with poor results.
7-27-42	The first British P-51 mission.
8-42	The P-38 draws its first blood. P-40Ks appear with a maximum speed of 363 miles per hour.
Late Summer '42	P-39s serve on Guadalcanal and in the Mediterranean.
9-42	The Army Air Force takes delivery of the A-36A, a dive-bombing version of the P-51. Its maximum speed is 356 miles per hour. XP-51B flight tests begin.
10-42	The P-51 becomes the first single-seat fighter based in England to penetrate the German border.
11-42	P-38Fs participate in large scale operations in North Africa. The P-38M appears.

1943

1943	P-40L production begins. Army Air Corps A-36As see combat in Sicily and Italy. Bf-109G production begins in high numbers.

	It reaches a maximum speed of 387 miles per hour, slower than the 109F.
Early '43	P-38s are in combat worldwide. P-47Ds leave the assembly line with a maximum speed of 433 miles per hour.
3-43	P-38H and P-51A deliveries begin. The Mustang achieves 390 miles per hour.
4-13-43	The first operational P-47B missions.
7-43	Long-range P-47C flights begin with a maximum speed of 433 miles per hour.
8-43	The improved A6M5 Zero appears with a maximum speed increased to 356 miles per hour. A total of 10,094 Zeros will be built by the end of the war. The P-38J appears, the fastest Lightning at 414 miles per hour. P-38s will claim more Japanese aircraft shot down than any other fighter.
12-1-43	P-51Bs are delivered to the Army Air Force.

1944

Early '44	The P-51B appears in Burma and Italy. Its maximum speed is 440 miles per hour.
2-44	Army Air Corps Airacobra strength peaks at 2,105 P-39s.
3-44	The P-40N appears with a maximum speed of 343 miles per hour. They are supplied to Russia, but Russian pilots do not favor them. They feel the P-39 can absorb more battle damage.
6-44	The P-38L appears.
7-24-44	The last P-39Q is built, ending total Airacobra production at 9,558 Airacobras.
8-44	All first line P-39 squadrons have re-equipped with other aircraft.
9-44	The P-47N flies with a maximum speed of 470 miles per hour. A total of 15,683 P-47s will eventually be built.
12-44	The last P-40N is assembled, ending Warhawk production at 13,738 P-40s.

1945

2-3-45	The P-51H achieves 487 miles per hour, 50 miles per hour faster than the P-51D, the highest produced Mustang variant.
4-7-45	P-51Ds undertake land-based strikes against Tokyo. A total of 14,819 Mustangs will eventually be built.
5-45	Germany surrenders and ends the war in Europe.
Summer '45	The night fighter P-38M appears.
8-45	Japan surrenders and ends the war in the Pacific.

From this survey it can be seen that the P-39 was always a faster fighter than the P-40 or the Japanese Zero. The P-39 was the fastest pursuit aircraft in the United States until the P-38 appeared. The P-39 was a year ahead of the P-38 in development, and four years ahead of the P-51. The final Airacobra model, the P-39Q, was only 11 miles per hour slower than the final Bf-109 model, the Bf-109G.

The 312th Fighter Squadron's P-39s, most likely a stateside training unit. BELL AIRCRAFT CORP. VIA TRUMAN A. PARTRIDGE, SR.

PERSONAL ACCOUNTS

While writing this history of the Airacobra, a goal was set to interview people who had "hands on" knowledge during the P-39's active flying years. The intention was to complete some research away from the library and speak directly with those who contributed to the Airacobra's fascinating legend. The author was extremely fortunate to interview the following people about their P-39 experiences. All interviews were taken by the author in 1990 with the person's full knowledge and permission and transcribed by the author. Editing was done for clarity. Through their personal accounts, we learn what it was to be associated with the unique Bell P-39 Airacobra. Here are their interviews presented in the order they were taken.

Photo taken in China in 1945.
COURTESY COLONEL JESSE D. MITCHELL, JR.

Photo taken in the 1970s.
COURTESY COLONEL JESSE D. MITCHELL, JR.

Colonel Jesse D. Mitchell, Jr.

P-40 and P-51 Fighter Pilot during World War Two.

During the summer of 1944, I was a Replacement Training Unit flying instructor. Our unit, the 502nd Fighter Squadron, was stationed at Punta Gorda Army Air Field in Florida, a rather primitive triangular shaped field located 25 miles north of Fort Myers. My job was training fighter pilots in the P-40N to fly formation, shoot aerial and ground gunnery and a myriad of other tasks for flying professionalism before they were assigned to an overseas flying unit.

On one hot, sultry afternoon, I led a flight of four P-40s on a formation and tactics mission. While at 8,000 feet flying through the Florida haze, I saw a flight of four fighter planes approaching from our two o'clock position. As they neared, I spread my flight to tactical spacing. I was surprised to see four P-39s drawing a pursuit curve on us!

During the next ten minutes, I experienced some of the wildest maneuvering in my 6,600 military flying hours. We tried every conceivable trick to gain a distinct advantage over the P-39s for a simulated gunnery attack. I had never mixed it up with P-39s before, and I was surprised they were so evenly matched with our P-40s.

After seeing a true advantage could not be gained and that my oil temperature was off the gauge at over 100 degrees Celsius, I reformed my flight of P-40s. After a wing waggle salute, we parted and returned to Punta Gorda.

(Jess Mitchell is the author's father. He later flew P-51s in China in 1945. After the war, he joined the Maryland Air National Guard where he flew fighters. He was the 175th Tactical Fighter Group's Commander from 1962 to 1976. He retired from the military in 1978.)

Mr. Joseph Cannon

Bell P-39 Test Pilot during World War Two.

Mr. Cannon had 39 years with Bell Aircraft Corporation and retired as their Director of Marketing in 1981.

Photo taken in 1985. COURTESY JOSEPH CANNON

Q. Mr. Cannon, when did you begin at Bell Aircraft, and what was your prior flying experience?

A: I was flying as an instructor in the Royal Canadian Air Force, but my hometown was Niagara Falls where the Bell plant was. A friend of mine and I decided we would see if we could get a job at Bell. We both did, and we were hired in 1942 in November. I was hired because I was flying multi-engine airplanes in the Royal Canadian Air Force. Our government was building the Bell bomber plant in Marietta, Georgia, to produce B-29s. From the time I was hired in November '42 until May '43, we flew P-39s (in Buffalo). Because we were waiting for the facility to be finished, we had the opportunity to fly production P-39s. I was not an experimental pilot at that time. I was actually a novice having never flown a fighter before. I went from multi-engine slow-speed training aircraft to the P-39. Within three weeks of my being hired, after ground school, I checked out in the P-39. To me, as a novice, the '39 was a doll! It was easy to fly because of its tricycle landing gear which I had never flown before. It was the only World War Two fighter that had a tricycle landing gear at the time. (I flew) production flight tests which were taking a new aircraft off the line, putting in a couple of flights, checking the "squawks" (complaints), then re-flying (the plane) after those squawks had been worked off. I got 500 to 600 hours in various production P-39s before we went to Marietta, Georgia (to fly B-29s). So, my '39 situation was rather short lived! We did come back to the (Buffalo) plant periodically from Marietta, but they had switched over to the P-63 which was an improved P-39 with a better engine, higher altitude capabilities, a better wing (and) better controllability. (It had) a little of everything better. During one of our trips back, we checked out in the P-59 which was the first jet airplane in the United States. By the time the war was over and we came back, there were no '39s except two under a Navy contract (which) were modified with swept wings (the L-39). We did some of the first swept wing research in the United States in 1946 with that airplane. (Note: The L-39s were actually P-63s).

Q: How old were you when you came to Bell in November 1942?

A: I was 22 or 23.

Q. How many prior flying hours in military aircraft did you have?

A: About 1,500 hours.

Q: Do you remember which P-39 models you flew?

A: Not really, although I do remember the "Q" in particular. I never flew the family of '39s delivered to the British which were known as the P-400. The '39s I flew had the 37mm (cannon) through the (propeller) hub and the .50s (machine guns) above and two pods outboard with .50s in each. That was the configuration.

Q: Did you test fire the P-39s?

A: Yes. We fired every tenth airplane, so we had a lot of fun! We had a floating target moared in Lake Ontario at the Niagara River off Old Fort Niagara, and we would fire at it. I particularly remember the low muzzle velocity of the 37 (mm cannon). You could see the shell come out of the cannon and lob in a very curving rajectory over the target which you could never hit. At east I could never hit it! You would sight the target, but then you brought the nose up because you knew the fall-off was so great you would fire short. I don't know how those guys hit tanks in Russia, but it turned out to be a great tank-killer.

Q: When you fired the fuselage machine guns and the cannon, did the cockpit fill with exhaust vapor?

A: I never noticed it. After the aircraft were in

service for a while and with the tough maintenance in the field, maybe some of the seals around the barrels got loose. That probably could happen, but the airplanes I flew were new, and no problem (was ever noticed).

Q: What was good about the P-39?

A: What was good was first, its marvelous ground handling capabilities, both from the standpoint of take-off and landing. (Second), it was the lightness of the controls; high roll rates (with) very light ailerons; a very maneuverable airplane. I think those were the good sides. It had a lot of bad sides, but the good sides were those.

Q: Please discuss the downside of the P-39.

A: I don't know anything about the so called "tumbling" story that went around for years. Bell's position was that the aircraft never tumbled. Maybe somebody could prove it, but we could never prove it tumbled. We felt it had an oscillatory spin capability that the nose rose and fell. As it rotated, it gave the *illusion* of tumbling, but we don't think it ever tumbled. I never got myself in a combat situation where that happened. I spun the airplane and I know how it spins, and maybe a good point is that you've got to work to make it spin. One problem was overheating. The engine required level flight to cool. Its glycol (coolant) system was marginal. If you didn't fire up, taxi and take off within about two minutes, you had to shut down because (it) boiled the glycol over. The cooling system was inadequate for prolonged ground handling. Once in flight, it cooled fine, and there was no problem. (The) second one was vibration. The reason for repeated (test) flights on production '39s was (for) what we called a "vibrator." What they (Bell) would do was re-index the shaft with the prop gearbox forward and the engine to give the prop the proper alignment, balance or what (ever) to minimize the vibration. Some were so bad (that) the instrument panel was a blur! It was a long (extension) shaft. It went between your legs, up forward and then into a reduction gearbox, this big box up forward, and the prop. It had semi-universals. The fuselage would flex even though it had box beams along the bottom longitudinally, (but) then things would get out of alignment. Then vibration would get in. I think that was probably always a problem. I suspect that as the airplanes got more hours and service time, the vibration became more. I don't know that, but I would suspect it. It wasn't smooth like a P-51, for instance, which had the prop attached to the front of the engine. (The P-39) always had some vibration. The third downside, although it really didn't have anything to do with flying the airplane, was its performance. It didn't have the performance it should have had. The early engine in the '39 was a single stage blower and it didn't do much above 15,000 feet. In some theatres that was a drawback, especially (against) the Japanese. The P-63 was getting better. To me (for) just flying the airplane, it went fast enough (and) was fine, but a fighter pilot, I'm sure, missed the horsepower and the extra blower to get to higher altitudes.

Q: Would the P-39 have been different had the supercharger been allowed on its Allison engine? Would it have been a better performer like the P-47 and the P-51?

A: Well, the '47 had a turbo on it, but it wasn't gear driven. The '47 was a brute force, heavy airplane. It was not a good fighter plane other than you could use brute force capabilities. You couldn't knock it out of the sky because it had so much armor. The '39 was a far superior fighter as far as maneuverability goes. I'm not sure (that) even with a P-63 engine in the '39 (it would have been a different airplane). The '63 would have been a credible airplane had it gotten into service (usage in our own military). It had the same type wing as the '51: a laminar flow, smooth, flush riveted wing. It would have been the more comparable airplane. Maybe the '39 had outlived its time.

Q: It has been stated the P-39 could absorb more than its fair share of battle damage?

A: Well, I heard stories about it. It was used by the Russians as a ground (attack) airplane most effectively. Armed with a cannon, it was a tank-buster. It flew at low altitudes because it couldn't fly high. The way they used it, it was a natural. I assume it had enough protective armor to be hard to knock down. It could have been developed as a ground-support airplane by putting in more strategically placed armor plate if that's what the mission was going to be. But that wasn't the mission it was built for. Whether the Russians changed the armor plate or put more armor on it, I don't know.

Q: What was the visibility from the airplane?

A: Absolutely fabulous! There are people that think you didn't have visibility. I can't understand that!

Q: May I ask how tall you are?

A: I'm 5'10".

Q: So you are about the height the P-39 was designed for?

A: That may be. I wouldn't have wanted to be 6'2" in the airplane. We had one guy that was tall. He couldn't wear a seat pack in the airplane. He wore a backpack. We wore seat packs that would put you in the position. You could see everything.

Q: What was the visibility looking toward the rear?

A: It was good. There was one problem. We had a radio which was a box about a foot by fifteen (inches) by fifteen mounted on the deck behind us. If that hadn't been there, we would have had beautiful rear visibility. The early '51s and the P-40s had horrible rear visibility. It was only when they put the bubble canopy on the '51 that you had good rearward visibility. The '47 had a bubble. I thought (the P-39) was pretty good.

Q: Did you fly any P-39s with photo-reconnaissance cameras?

A: No, I did not.

Q: Did you last fly the P-39 in March '43?

A: No. In the mid-Fifties, along about '57 or '58, a woman called Larry Bell, so it had been before Larry died. That would have been '56. She had an airplane called *Galloping Gertie.*

Q: That P-39 is at the National Air and Space Museum!

A: Yes, it is! I'm working on a committee for an air and space museum here, the Niagara Frontier (Museum). She called Bell. At that time (her P-39) wasn't at the Air and Space Museum. She had it.

Q: Was that a lady named Betty Haas Pfister?

A: I guess it is Pfister. She brought that airplane to Bell and left it. I flew it to the storage hangar in Chicago. That was the last I heard of that airplane. Recently, (while) working in the museum, she has been in contact with us again, but has decided not to donate it to the Niagara Frontier (Museum). That's the last '39 I flew.

Q: Had that P-39 been maintained well?

A: Yes. It was in good shape. We had two '39s for the 1946 Cleveland Air Races, but we lost one. One was flown by Tex Johnston the first year, and he cleaned up. The second year it was flown by a friend of mine named Jay Demming, but that airplane lost twice because the big Corsairs with the "corncob" engines were surplused. That airplane (the Corsair) was (a) brute force, and it just cleaned up at the Cleveland unlimited races.

Q: Did you ever see Cobra I *and* Cobra II *close up?*

A: Yes. They were modified in summer 1946 in our flight test hangar where I worked. I was familiar with the work that went on. I was at the lake when Jack Woolams unfortunately ploughed in with ship I.

Q: Were they semi-officially company sponsored by Bell Aircraft?

A: Bell would liked to have sponsored them and wanted the publicity, but we had a sub-company organized to do the work. The people that worked on the airplanes worked for this sub-company.

Q: Skylanes?

A: Skylanes Unlimited. It was a vehicle that could take the responsibility and the insurance, and leave it out of Bell's hands. That's the way Larry wanted it.

Q: Did Mr. Bell allow access to the company's technical resources?

A: Yes.

Q: Did you fly Cobra I *or* Cobra II?

A: No, I did not. One interesting thing (was that) we stripped them. We worked with Allison (Engine Company) who was (using the planes as) a showplace for the Allison engine. They souped it up, and we developed awful nice horsepower. (We) put a bigger prop on to soak up the horsepower. Once you put the bigger prop on, you develop some torque you wouldn't believe! You had to fly the airplane, the boys tell me, with hard right rudder practically all the time, just standing on the rudder, to take that torque. That wasn't the case with the '39 as it was designed.

Q: Were Cobra I *and* Cobra II *fitted with different lightweight doors?*

A: You could crank up the windows in the P-39 and the '63 like a car. That and the inner liner were removed to lighten them up. I don't think they built other doors. They stripped away material from the existing doors.

Q: Did you like the P-39's door design as opposed to a sliding canopy?

A: It was novel! I liked it. You could pull the handle and the door would come loose on its hinges. Then you had a wide open space. I never had to bail out, but it would be a very easy airplane to get out of.

Q: Were the window roll-up mechanisms similar to an auto's?

A: Yes, just like an auto.

Q: Any problem with sealing the windows? Did they leak or whistle?

A: I don't remember. It was so noisy inside you couldn't tell. I mean it was *noisy* from the engine and gearbox!

Q: If you flew the P-39 for longer than a few hours, would the vibration fatigue your legs?

A: No. It never bothered me. Again, our airplanes were in a lot better shape, smoother and better maintained.

Q: How long did you work at Bell Aircraft?

A: I retired in '81. I had 39 years with Bell. I ran Flight Test until '58 and then got into marketing since I was almost in the marketing game anyway. You're so close to the products. I became Director of Marketing. I was in marketing the last 15 to 20 years, and (then) I got out. I haven't flown an airplane in ten years. It was about fifty-fifty: half my career in Flight Test and half my career trying to peddle things!

Q: Were there any places where P-39s were test flown away from populated areas?

A: Yes, over Lake Ontario along the shoreline. Niagara Falls is nine miles from the shore of Lake Ontario. We would fly north of the airport (where) you wouldn't fly over 14 or 15 houses. You could go to the firing range. We were over open territory. We didn't fly over the Falls much, except for a few brave souls who flew under the bridge, but most of it was to the north.

Q: Were there any auxiliary fields used for emergencies?

A: There were small fields around, (but) I don't remember our airplanes having to land in an emergency on a satellite field. That may have happened. Buffalo was 20 miles away and easily reachable, even in a glide if you lost an engine. There were a few emergency landings at the Buffalo airport, but I don't remember any small fields nearby where anybody went.

Q: Was there an average air time a new P-39 was flown for flight test?

A: Yes. The duration of a test flight was about one hour. There were a few (of) what were called "one hoppers." Most (new P-39s) had two or three (test) flights. Some had as many as five when we had a vibration problem. You got a total from the very best airplanes (of) maybe an hour to as many as five hours on the worst airplanes. Somebody may have the statistics, but I don't.

Q: Were there test pilots who flew the "shakers" who were better for correcting the vibration problem?

A: Hard to say; I don't know. We (Bell) were building (new P-39s) at about seven or eight a day when I left. The massive inputs from lots of airplanes and flights were done after I was gone.

Q: Why is the P-39 unfavorably remembered by aviation writers when the facts do not substantiate such negative feeling?

A: I have an idea (it is due to) its lack of performance. We were fighting a sophisticated enemy on the German side and on the Japanese side. They (had) airplanes that were light and maneuverable. If the '47 had been around to fight in the Pacific theatre, it would have been a failure with the airplanes it was fighting. But it turned out to be a great airplane in the European theatre. It was (the P-39's) lack of performance. Nobody could groan about its handling capabilities and its tricycle gear which were fabulous. Maybe it didn't have enough firepower. The 37mm was not the right gun for air-to-air combat. It's probably its armament and its performance.

Q: Did any American-made airplane perform the ground-attack role better?

A: I don't know enough about it. I don't know the ground strafing story of the P-39, except I don't think there were any low-level operations in Europe with P-39s.

Thank you, Mr. Cannon.

Lieutenant Colonel William A. Shomo

P-39 Fighter Pilot in World War Two.

Lieutenant Colonel William A. Shomo flew P-39s, P-40s and F-6Ds, the photo-reconnaissance version of the P-51D, during World War Two. He is an ace and Medal of Honor winner as a result of his exploits flying the Mustang. On one Mustang mission on January 11, 1945, Colonel Shomo shot down a Japanese bomber and six Japanese fighters within a fifteen-minute period.

Photo taken on March 5, 1944, on Dobodura, Papua New Guinea, with the first "Snooks," when Colonel Shomo was a Second Lieutenant.
COURTESY TRUMAN A. PARTRIDGE, SR.

Q: Lieutenant Colonel Shomo, please briefly review your military career before we discuss the P-39?

A: I went into the flying cadet program in 1940 in Class 42-C, graduating from Brooks Field in San Antonio, Texas. I went to primary at Tulsa, Oklahoma where Spartan Aeronautics was located, and then went to basic at Randolph. (I) went to Brooks Field and completed the advanced training. From that for about six months I wound up on coastal patrol at the Gulf of Mexico flying O-47s (observation planes) and L-4 Piper Cubs. After we left, we were transferred to another (Air) National Guard observation unit and moved to Louisiana. (We) joined the 71st Group which consisted of a B-25 (medium bomber) squadron, two P-39 squadrons and an L-5 squadron, which was the more advanced version of the L-4 used for artillery spotting. We left there and went overseas. After two years overseas, (I) came home and got out. I was going through premedical training to become a doctor which I wanted before I went into the service. After about 18 months, I got a letter from General Kenney (Major General George C. Kenney who had been the air commander in the southwest Pacific during World War Two) who was the commanding general of the Strategic Air Command at Andrews Field (in Maryland). I had known him in the Pacific Theatre as MacArthur's commanding general of the air forces. He asked me if I was interested in a regular commission and said I could have one. My last board was coming up in three weeks. I said okay. I missed flying and I went back to the regular Air Force. (I) finished 28½ years and got out in 1968 when I retired.

Q: Did you first fly the P-39 with the 71st Tactical Reconnaissance Squadron?

A: Yes. I checked out on (the P-39) two months before, it and the P-40, before we went to the 71st Tac Recon Wing. They had a sub-depot at Lake Pontchartrain Field in New Orleans where we were assigned out of flying school. Before we got there, (the Army) shipped the (prior) P-39 outfit to England. They left some P-39s and P-40s at the sub-depot to be repaired. After they were repaired, they had no one to test top (test fly) them. I talked them into letting me test top them. One of our line chiefs showed me how to start the P-39, and I let her go! I managed to get it up and down without smashing it, and I was now what they called a "hot pilot" in those days! I wound up going to the 71st, which was P-39s, with the 82nd Tac Recon Squadron. (I) flew the P-39 until we wound up overseas. We flew the P-39 for a year after it was declared obsolete, even for training in the United States. We were supposed to get the P-63, the Bell Kingcobra, over in New Guinea, (but) they never got there. The P-39 had a very short range. We needed more range to get where the air war was. We never got the P-63s; they didn't develop the range difference they were supposed to; so we kept flying the P-39s. There was a squadron of P-40s the Aussies (Australians) had. They parked them at Biak Island (northwest of New Guinea) when they got a squadron of (British) Spitfires by aircraft carrier from England. They turned them over to the Aussies, and they became a night fighter outfit. We got to use, on a one for one basis, the war-weary P-40s they had parked for a couple months after they got their Spitfires. We were flying what was left. Most were called a "bunch of spare parts flying (in) close formation," but they were simply all that was available to us.

Q: How many hours could you fly the P-39 on a flight?

A: The P-39 was good for two hours and 20 minutes according to the tech order on a flight. We found by throwing the book away how to lean those things out. We took the idiot control off (which) was a coordinating gimmick that when you used your throttle, it automatically coordinated the mixture changes. That was a very costly way of operating that engine (for) gas consumption. We had the crewchiefs yank them out. We manually operated the mixture controls. On one mission (with) 16 airplanes out of Biak (Island), we were up 3 hours and 16 minutes according to the Tech Rep's report. We had a Bell Aircraft Tech Rep in our squadron, and he sent that information on his mission reports. They sent a letter and told him he better quit drinking that jungle juice! One airplane wouldn't stay in the air that long let alone 16 flying in combat formation!

Q: Was that while carrying a belly tank?

A: Yes. (For the) P-38s at the same base we were at and the P-47 units, they could go out for five hours on a flight and have time to fight and come back. They could go out farther than we could and reach where the Japanese were located. As we moved closer to them (the Japanese), they would move back. We never had enough range in the P-39 to get where the air war was. It was 16 months before I saw a Japanese airplane in the air while I was in a position to put a (gun) sight on him. The rest of the time I never saw any Japanese or was lucky enough to stumble onto them. There were two pilots in that 16 months that ran into some Japanese airplanes. One was a Japanese version of the DC-2 called a (Mitsubishi Ki-57 twin-engine) "Topsy," and another one was a dive bomber, a "Val." They were both shot down by our pilots. They just happened to stumble on to them. We were too far away to get where the aerial fighting was. The 475th Fighter Group, for example, (would) take off (with P-38s) from Dobodura (in southeastern New Guinea). They would fly to Hollandia (northern New Guinea) on one engine, (then) turn both on, fight for 15 or 20 minutes, shut the other one down, and come back on the opposite engine. That was their idea how to get the most cruise out of the airplane. That's when (Charles) Lindbergh came. He was an expert on long range navigation and cruise control. He showed how to get another hour and a half out of the (P-38) (when) they thought they were getting every minute out of it. We were too far away from the air war, but the 475th would go up with a group, that's three squadrons, of P-38s. They would figure on having no less than 75 Japanese airplanes in the air at one time. They had plenty of targets, and they were getting where they could reach them. We couldn't do that. I had, in terms of hours of flying time, close to 400 hours with the P-39.

January 31, 1944, at Dobodura, Papua New Guinea. Members of the 82nd Tactical Reconnaissance Squadron, with Lieutenant William A. Shomo standing on the far left. His crew chief, Staff Sergeant Ralph Winkle, is sitting third from the left on the wing.
COURTESY TRUMAN A. PARTRIDGE, SR.

Q: Did you encounter the enemy in the air while flying the P-39?

A: No, not in the P-39. I regret I never did because I was convinced I could shoot down anything that flew with that airplane.

Q: How would you assess the P-39's firepower?

A: There are few airplanes, even today, that come close to what that airplane was capable of. We had 31 one-pound 37mm cannon shells which fired through the prop hub. That thing (the fired shells) had a definite rainbow trajectory being so heavy (with) a small shell propelling it. If you learned to use that gun properly, you could drop (the shell) right in a pickle barrel or somebody's shirt pocket walking along the beach with no problem. I used to take the new pilots out because they had been told in the States by gunnery instructors that (with) the cannon, you couldn't hit anything! When they came over, they were convinced it was no good. I used to take new pilots (and) fly up and down the beaches. I would tell them to watch. I'd make a slow pass (and fire at) point blank range with the cannon and prove you could be very accurate with that gun if you didn't fire it like a .50 caliber machine gun because it didn't have a flat trajectory. We (had) quite a bit of steel barge traffic. The Japanese used to resupply from ships off shore. They would load the barges as it got dark. When they got loaded, they would have 15 or 20 in a string heading for shore from five or ten miles out. The Class A barge carried 75 fully armed troops or 6,000 rations, that is, enough rations for 6,000 troops (for) one day. It was an important load and an important target from the standpoint of stopping the resupply. We would catch these barges before dark three or four miles off shore and plant a cannon shell at the base of the steering housing in the back of the barge. It would blow the bottom of the barge out. The fuel tanks were beside the steering column. In ten seconds, the barge would disappear into the ocean! It was a very effective weapon. We used it on larger boats in shipping with the same results. That thing was a tremendous weapon. You had six machine guns with it if you wanted to have that firepower.

Q: Was 37mm cannon prone to jamming?

A: Yes, they would, but you (had) mechanical charging like a pistol grip you just simply squeezed, pulled back and shoved the next shell in. You could clear a jam instantly. We had some problem with jamming, but generally they were more than effective. Our biggest problem was we ran out of ammunition before we ran out of targets! We had "targets of opportunity." We would be driving up the shoreline, plotting (Japanese) escape trails, shooting trucks, tanks and whatever they were moving with (and) finding out where their motor pools were. We'd be working them over. If we could reach their older airports like Madang and Saidor, Finschhaffen, Lae and Nadzab, we'd catch their aircraft (on the ground). They would bring them in before dark from farther back and land, refuel, take off and hit our closer bases about 8:30 or 9:00 at night, and (then) they (would) turn around. That's where you get the "washing machine Charlie" name from. About 8:30 this one "Betty" (Japanese bomber) would come in every night (with) the same direction and time, drop bombs in our search lights, and (then) make a 180-degree turn, come back across the field, and go home. We would catch these aircraft once in awhile on the ground at the airports they were staging through. We could get credit for anything on the ground. I got credit for 29 on the ground.

Q: What did you like about the P-39?

A: I'm one of the few who actually loved the P-39. That airplane had a tremendously unwarranted reputation. Everybody seemed to add to the negative things said about it. Whether they were true or not didn't matter. But that airplane, as far as I'm concerned, was one of the finest airplanes ever built. For the purpose it was used, if you were under 15,000 feet, I don't think anything could touch it. I wouldn't have hesitated to take on a whole squadron of P-38s with it below 15,000 feet. I would have a fighting chance of knocking them down because they couldn't touch (me) with the maneuverability. If you kept your airspeed above 300 miles per hour, the Japanese couldn't touch you with the Zero (fighter). They couldn't turn inside you with a Zero if you kept your airspeed around 300 or better. The control surfaces on the Zero, as light as it was, didn't have hydraulic actuators. They would get up around 300 miles an hour and the pressures on their control surfaces (were) too heavy to overcome with manual action, and (they became) very difficult to maneuver. They (the Zeros) were always trying to get you to drop your airspeed when you (fought) them. The same was true with the P-38 and the P-47. They outmaneuvered the Japanese Zero when they could keep their airspeed above 300. The guys who got shot down in the P-38 or P-47 were the guys who let their airspeed fall. That enabled the Zero to outmaneuver them. As long as they kept their airspeed up, the Zero couldn't touch them.

Q: How would you assess the downside of the P-39?

A: There was one supposed downside that you may have heard about. Did you ever hear of a P-39 "tumbling"? That was the greatest myth ever. The P-39 did not tumble. When you were watching it from a half a mile, it looked like it was tumbling end over end. Before we went overseas, we were sent through a P-39 overseas combat training unit. They had students who (had) bailed out or just rode them in that supposedly got in tumbles. It got to where the pilots had flatly refused to fly them. Every time somebody augered it (crashed), a couple more would say, "unh-uh, that's it. I'm not gonna fly it." I had a guy who went through flight school with me by the name of Dick Clawn. He and I loved that airplane. We started experimenting to see (for ourselves). First, we talked to the pilots who had the so-called tumble or bailed out. (We) read a number of the flight safety accident investigation reports. Every one said the same thing. They simply couldn't control it. You had to either accept you were going to auger in in a flat spin or the equivalent, or you were to bail out before it got too low. We were able to duplicate this so called "tumble", and we did it many, many times. We stayed above 10,000 feet because it was obvious (based on) these reports and (from) talking to the other pilots that if you were above 6,000 feet when you went into this so called tumble, you had no problem getting out. If you were below 6,000 feet, it wasn't good to stay with (it). They came with an order based on Dick Clawn's and my checking the airplane (after) convincing our flight supervisors we knew what we were talking about. (It) was a series of rapid whip stalls in one direction and another direction, and when you're off a half a mile (or) you're watching from the ground, it looked like the P-39 was going end over end; nose and tail, nose and tail; but it wasn't. The distance precluded seeing what it was doing. The moment everybody saw it flip-flopping around, they said, "hey, there goes another tumble!" We proved that you had to be above 6,000 feet (and) turn the airplane loose when you went into one. We had no problem putting them into the tumble; that was simple. All you do (is) pull it down in a loop and get your airspeed up. Pull it up with full throttle vertically, and pull over. Fly upside down until almost flat on your back horizontally. At that point, with full power, snap the stick back in your gut and hold it. It would flip into what looked like end over end, but it was a series of whip stalls. (After) you watched the horizon go in all directions: it would come from your right knee one time, the next time from the back of your helmet down in front of your face, and the next time it would come from the left knee on the right side. You never got the same picture where the horizon was which proved it wasn't going end over end. At that point, you turned the stick loose, chopped the throttle and let the stick, the rudder and everything go, and you just folded your arms and sat there. Within about 2,000 or 2,500 (feet) maximum, the nose would quit spiralling in a tight

Lieutenant Colonel William A. Shomo wearing his Medal of Honor. COURTESY TRUMAN A. PARTRIDGE, SR.

vertical spin. (The P-39) would level out in a flat spin. The nose would drop down in a tight spiral. Then it would stop and gradually fly out of that vertical spiral going down. You (would) take over (the) controls and pour the coal to it. But if you fought the controls and tried to bring it out, you just kept coming down in these whip stalls. You didn't have (large) enough control surfaces in relation to the size and weight of the airplane to override this series of whip stalls. You had to wait until it aerodynamically settled down by going into this fairly flat spin, nose down tightening spiral, and then let it fly itself out. It would take its own needs for control, and it would come out. They sent factory reps and test pilots from Bell Aircraft to make training movies of our work before we left. They used those to prove to the pilots flying P-39s (in) the schools that the (P-39s) were perfectly safe. That was the only downside other than the short range. They had (another) possible downside. That was the armor. (The P-39) had, for example, a chunk of belly armor under the seat that weighed 750 pounds. We wanted more speed and maneuverability, (and) we wanted more range. We started peeling armor plate off the belly first, taking the idiot controls off, (and) doing things that would make the airplane capable. We've historically in the United States made the same mistake with every airplane built, and we make it today. We build a beautiful fighter like a P-51, and then we started hanging stuff on it. We did it with the P-39 and the P-40. (We) keep hanging safety features on it; emergency systems backing up emergency systems. The weight factor uses up your maneuverability. If you could take these (extra) pieces out, that airplane would fly like a bumble bee, and it really worked! After we got them lightened up, I left Nadzab in New Guinea (and) ran into my cousin who had been there for three years in the Army Air Corps (in) Military Airlift as a clerk. He was a college graduate. He was as frustrated as anybody could be because they had no idea when they were going home. There was no stateside return policy. I got the idea (that because) he was crazy about airplanes, I said, "How would you like to take a ride in this airplane?" while I was showing it to him on the line. He said, "Yeah, that would be great!" We took the 'chute out (as) you sat on your 'chute and emergency pack. The cockpit in a P-39 is one of the smallest. He weighed about 125 pounds, and I weighed 145. I sat on the seat, he sat on my lap, and I didn't put the shoulder harness over. I put the seat belt across our laps and fastened it, and we took off! As far as I know nobody ever had two people on board a P-39 prior to that! Being in the jungle, we could get away with just about anything, and I wasn't above trying it!

I took him north of Nadzab. I knew some escape trails where there were still Japanese using (them) during daylight hours to get away from where they were unable to get supplies and trying to escape to rejoin their own forces. We found some Japanese along this escape trail. (I) showed him how to operate the gun and cannon, and he had a ball! We ran across a machine gun nest, an ack-ack (anti-aircraft) nest, protecting this escape trail. By coming in at an angle we were able to make a flat pass and dump the ammo into it! Incidentally, I made a remark earlier that wasn't quite true. I said, "and there were six machine guns on it." I was thinking of the P-51 when I said that. We had the P-39Q and the P-39N. The N model; both of them had the 37mm cannon; earlier models had a 20mm cannon, like the P-39F; but the N and the Q model had the 37mm cannon in the nose. They had two .50s (calibre machine guns) on the top of the nose. Then they had on the N model two .30 calibres in each wing firing outside the prop arc. You had four .30s in that one, plus two .50s in the nose, plus a cannon. In the Q model, you had the same thing: a 37mm cannon in the nose, two .50s on the top of the nose, and instead of the four .30s in the wing, they put a fairing around a .50 calibre machine gun under each wing in place of the four .30s. That gave you four .50s on that bird and a 37mm cannon. That was the difference between the Q and the N models.

Q: Please compare the P-39 with the P-40.

A: I flew the P-40 almost as much as the P-39. For a while we were equipped with both, and both (were) "war-weary." The P-40 was a great bird, but it had that long nose in front. It did not have the maneuverability of the P-39, (but) it was maneuverable. If you kept your airspeed up, you could outfly a Japanese Zero. Our people in southeast Asia were able to prove that during the early war. The P-40 was a good airplane except it didn't have a cannon. It had an almost identical range as the P-39, (but) it was a rather awkward design from the standpoint of trying to get any real increase in maneuverability.

Q: What was the visibility from the P-39?

A: It was excellent. The P-39 had two doors, one on each side, that were automobile doors. They had automobile wind-up windows.

Q: What about the rear visibility?

A: You could look past your tail. They did have radio equipment behind, but that was no interference.

Q: Were your P-39s equipped for photo-reconnaissance?

A: We never had camera equipment in (our) airplanes. What they were referring to was when we were on our way over to the Pacific. Before we got there, General Kenney found that this Tactical Reconnaissance Squadron and a night fighter squadron of P-61s (a twin-engine fighter plane) were coming to join his forces. He said, "I can use the night fighters, but I can't afford to have whatever this Tactical business (is)." He didn't know what it was! It was something new as far as they were concerned. Not knowing what they were, he said, "Turn that boat around and take it back to California and dump them off because I'm not going to have them over here burning up my gas when I need it for straight fighters. I haven't got enough now." They finally got it settled! We crawled off 31 days later at Milne Bay (at the southeast tip) in New Guinea, and that's when we found we were getting P-39s. We went to Port Moresby. Here was a squadron of P-39s parked on the edge of the Seven Mile Strip (in Jackson) in the hills. The 80th Fighter Squadron had gotten P-38s. They parked the P-39s, rolled the windows up, put some chocks on (the wheels), and let them sit. They had been sitting (for) three (to) almost four months by the time we got there. Nobody had touched them. There weren't any mechanics. They left a supply sergeant with his tool box and C-rations to wait until whomever came to get the airplanes could sign for them. Then he could rejoin (his) outfit over the mountains at Dobodura. When we got there, we couldn't get them started! We worked for two weeks, (the) pilots mind you (as we) had no mechanics. We had screwdrivers and pliers this staff sergeant had in his toolbox, and we started working. We finally got them working on both mags (magnetos) in most cases. We were able to take off, make a quick flight around the field and land, and we parked them until we'd get the next one finished. We got these airplanes at least working on one mag pretty reliably, (because when) we took off, we had to clear the Owen Stanley Mountain Range between Port Moresby going east to Dobodura which was where we were going to operate. We had to get up to 14,000 feet to get over the Owen Stanley Mountains. We scraped a few bottoms on those things before we crossed that mountain!

Q: Have one of your P-39s been restored?

A: Yes. It is in Buffalo at the Naval and Servicemen's Museum. That's where the airplane was made, of course, at the Bell Aircraft Company in Buffalo.

Q: Is that Snooks *or* Snooks 2nd?

A: That one was *Snooks 2nd. Snooks the first* got battered. One pilot flew it on an altered mission. We had to swap planes until we got them all working. One pilot flew it. He came back and had some problems. He banged up the landing gear, and I had to get another airplane. It wound up being *Snooks 2nd. Snooks* was the name on the right side, up front. Traditionally the crewchief had the right side of the airplane for whatever he wanted on it, and the pilot had the left. We didn't have time to put anything there. The crewchief took some whitewash and painted *Snooks 2nd* on the right side before my first mission. That was all that was on it. The other airplanes I flew had the moniker of the *Flying Undertaker.* That's what I was before I went into World War Two.

Q: When did you last see Snooks 2nd *before learning it had been recovered?*

A: I hadn't seen it since 1944. They parked them at Aitape in (north central) New Guinea below Hollandia on the jungle strip along with P-40s. They sat there rotting from early '45. I saw this airplane in 1981. I got a call from a commercial artist named Truman Partridge who said he was restoring this airplane for the Naval Museum, and it had been brought from the Pacific. They picked up a bunch of rusted planes. Some restauranteur in California (David Tallichet) picked about 27; a group of P-40s and P-39s. (He) brought them out, put them on a boat, brought them to the United States and was gradually restoring these so he could put an airplane in front of his restaurants on the west coast. He wanted to put one (a restaurant) in Buffalo, and they talked him into donating this P-39 to this Naval Museum which was getting started. He (had) agreed to give a P-40. They went from Buffalo (and) picked up this airplane. (They) took the wing on flat beds and brought it back. They started cleaning up the rusted pieces. (They) found identification numbers, and they started checking back. They went to the Bell Aircraft plant. (Bell) had put all their engineering data, drawings and records on all P-39s built in one hangar at the end of the war. As things would happen, the hangar burned! There were no records at Bell Aircraft Company on these aircraft. They went through the Pentagon and Wright-Patterson (Air Force Base), a few other places and some of the old sub-depots where they (P-39s) were overhauled, and they finally tracked that this bird had been assigned to my squadron and that it was my airplane! That's when they called me, and that's the first I had heard about it. They got it restored outside. They built a $500,000 building with this airplane as a centerpiece. They did a very meticulous and beautiful job restoring it, but they haven't got all the insides of it. They had a grand opening. I went when my squadron had its first reunion in conjunction with unveiling this P-39.

Q: Do you have any final comments about the P-39?

A: There were very few pilots compared to the total trained by the United States that got to fly the P-39 extensively or in combat. (The Army Air Force) was trying to phase the P-39 out in the States and overseas because of its short range. I don't know how familiar you are with the Lend-Lease program with the Russians. (The United States) started turning (over) P-39s and P-63s (which) were flown to Alaska. They had pilots (who) flew them to Russia. They loved the P-39. There was a Russian squadron (commander) during the German attack on the Russian front called Pokryshkin. He was flying a squadron of P-39s when the Germans made their mass attacks on the Russian front. Hitler was going to bury the Russians. They inundated Russia with dive bombers, troop transports, and were just wreaking havoc. Along came Pokryshkin with his P-39 squadron to slow the attacks on the more important targets. Pokryshkin shot down 59 German airplanes in (air) battles, and he was flying P-39s. He had victories in other types, too. He painted his P-39 very distinctively so it could be recognized in the air by the Germans. Every time he was spotted by the Germans leading the P-39 squadron, the cry would go out from the Germans, "Achtung, Pokryshkin!" and that was all they needed to say! In a number of cases, the Germans turned around because they didn't want to tangle with Pokryshkin nor his squadron. It was because of the effectiveness of the P-39. In my personal opinion, it was one of the greatest airplanes built. I'd give my right arm if I could have one for the pleasure of flying. They were a tremendous piece of equipment.

Thank you, Lieutenant Colonel Shomo.

(Lieutenant Colonel Shomo was interviewed in March 1990. He passed away on June 25, 1990.)

Mr. Frank "Chick" Lajudice

Crew chief in 1946 for Cobra II—*the Airacobra that won the Thompson Trophy Race*

Today, Mr. Lajudice manages the flight training program for Bell Helicopters/TEXTRON in Fort Worth, Texas.

Q: Mr. Lajudice, when did you begin at Bell Aircraft?

A: I started at Bell on July 20, 1941.

Q: What were your duties?

A: My first job was unloading machine guns out of box cars. The next day, I disassembled the machine guns, degreased them and reassembled the guns into left hand and right hand machine guns. Then I started installing machine guns in (P-39) fuselages and wings on the airplanes at the Elmwood plant. Then, in late August or the first of September, I went to the Niagara Falls plant. They were just opening. I took the first fuselage. We set it on the end of the assembly line. We went through the twelve stations to assemble it. When we got to the end of the line, we assembled the wings; installed the guns, synchronized and bore-sighted them; and we followed that fuselage outside to the ground-runs area. From that day I was on the end of the assembly line, installing machine guns; synchronizing, bore-sighting, firing them in the gun butts; engine testing the engine, and getting (the P-39s) ready for flight. Then in the middle of '42, they started a Bell Training School. (They) took the Cataract Hotel to teach army personnel about the P-39. I transferred to training the soldiers about synchronizing, bore-sighting the guns, and the engine. After about six or seven months, I transferred

Mr. Lajudice is on the far right of this photo taken on April 8, 1989, at the Confederate Air Force's 50th anniversary celebration of the P-39. To the far left is Mr. Ed Roseler of Bell Helicopter/TEXTRON; Col. "Sandy" Sansing of the CAF; Col. John Stokes, the CAF sole sponsor of the P-39; and Col. Ralph Boyce of the CAF. COURTESY BELL HELICOPTER/TEXTRON

to the service department and went in the field on the P-39s. I worked (at) Wright Field, Patterson Field and even at Eglin in Florida where we ran the tests on the P-39. I was with just about every station on the P-39. I travelled the country (as) a service rep. Then I spent a year in the Marine Corps. After I got out in early '46, I went back to Bell. That's when I got on the (racing) P-39 (program). We took two P-39s, stripped them and went to the Cleveland Air Races. In 1946 we won when Tex Johnston was the pilot. Slick Goodlin, who flew the (X-1) rocket aircraft, was the backup pilot. Jack Woolams was another (test) pilot, but he was killed before the (Cleveland) Air Race.

Q: Did the P-39 "tumble"?

A: That was one thing we had wrong. You have to realize (that) during the war; it's just like we (Bell) hired people to be mechanics that used to be driving milk trucks; we (the Army Air Corps) were getting young kids and making pilots out of them. They got in (pilot) training and (went) from a small airplane to a P-39, and they got out doing maneuvers. The P-39 got the reputation (for tumbling) but it was never ever proven, because I was on that program. People said they tumbled the airplane, (but) no one ever tumbled it. The thing they did get into when they got into a high-speed stall (was that) the airplane whipped down nose first so fast and flipped over that it seemed like tumbling. It knocked you from one side of the cockpit to the other, but it never tumbled. It was a high-speed stall. I was on that program. It never, ever tumbled, but it got the reputation.

Q: Would the P-39 have been a better airplane had the turbo-supercharger been allowed?

A: The P-39 was designed for (use as) a defensive airplane. The cannon (and) the guns (were) for ground-attack, which when we were on our defensive was a good airplane. It was a very good plane in Russia because they couldn't go to altitude. It was a good low-altitude airplane. When the war changed and you had to go to altitude and go for distance, no, the P-39 was sort of obsolete. The P-40 was (also) starting to get obsolete. They (Bell) put auxiliary fuel tanks on, but they never did get the altitude and distance, not until the P-63. (On) the P-63 we put a supercharger, but that was toward the end of the war. But (the P-39) was what it was designed for, for defense air (support).

Q: Was the cooling system prone to overheating on a warm day before the pilot took off?

A: Yes. On a warm day, if you sat and ran for a long time, there wasn't enough air going underneath the aircraft. The intakes were (only) large enough to let the air go through. Once you were moving, you had sufficient cooling because we had an adjustable door. Yes, it would overheat, and the Prestone (coolant) would get hot just sitting.

Q: Did the P-39's cannon have a low muzzle velocity requiring the pilot to arc the shot?

A: With the 37mm, the muzzle velocity was less than 1,000 feet per minute. It was a good gun, (but) it wasn't fast firing. It carried explosive shells designed for tanks, cars (and) trucks, (and) it was very good. Then we ended with a 20mm in the nose. The 20mm's muzzle velocity was better, the gun was more accurate, and you fired more shells. The Russians liked the 37mm cannon, (but) the British liked the 20mm.

Q: Did the P-39's extension shaft increase the life of its Allison engine?

A: (In) most airplanes, the prop and the gearbox are mounted on the front of the engine. The engine would take the vibration from the prop. The engines in the P-39s were behind the pilot, and (they) had no vibration from the propeller. Yes, it got by better. Especially (as compared to) an airplane like a P-40 with a gearbox up front. Your leaks were worse. It (the Allison) was a different engine when you mounted the prop on the engine. We had no problem with that engine on vibration.

Q: What was good about the P-39?

A: I liked the streamlining. The tricycle gear was the first put on an airplane at the time, and it was very good taxiing. The pilot had a very good view in the front. It wasn't like landing, taking off or taxiing an airplane (with) a conventional gear. With a conventional gear you had to go back and forth and look out each side of the window. In the P-39 you didn't have to go through that for taxiing, landing and taking off. I don't think you could beat it.

Q: Did the nose gear suffer after rough field handling?

A: They had a couple incidents. When you were operating off the dirt, the nose wheel would bounce. It would sometimes shimmy, but it never gave any big trouble. It was a electrically operated landing gear. It didn't have trouble (with) hydraulic leaks. I don't think we had more trouble with that landing gear than with other aircraft.

Q: Let's review your racing days after the war with Cobra I *and* Cobra II. *Were you employed by Skylanes Unlimited?*

A: No, I was with Bell Aircraft in Buffalo. Slick Goodlin, Tex Johnston and Jack Woolams set up a different company. It was Skylanes Unlimited. (They) formed that company and bought two P-39s for the Cleveland Air Race.

Q: Were you the crewchief for Cobra II?

A: I crewed Tex Johnston's airplane which won. Art Kreegie was crewing Jack Woolams' airplane. (Woolams) was our chief test pilot. He (Kreegie) was on *Cobra I*, and I had *Cobra II*. During the Cleveland Air Races, Jack Woolams, when he was on (his) time trials, got detonation in his engine. When he got back, we checked the plugs and everything seemed right. He said, "We have time, let's change the engine." Jack Woolams flew to Buffalo (in *Cobra I*). We had some mechanics in Buffalo. They changed the engine. The following day when Jack was testing the engine, he went over Lake Ontario. (He) was making a speed run when the windshield blew in, and he got killed. He flew into the lake. Art Kreegie who was crewing *Cobra I* and I stayed on *Cobra II* and finished the air race three days later.

Q: Were the windows in Cobra II *original or was other glass used? How changed were the planes?*

A: On both aircraft, *Cobra I* and *Cobra II*, we stripped all armor plate. We yanked the plate underneath and the armor by the nose gear box. We took out 1,800 pounds of weight including the self-sealing fuel tanks. On the airplanes (there was) two inch armor plate glass over the pilot's face. We took that out, and in doing so, made some reinforcement to hold the (front) window. The reinforcement we did held the window, but the two side windows caused the trouble. They sucked out. Then the front broke, and that killed Jack Woolams. It was the side windows around the canopy. On the other one (*Cobra II*), we put a brace on the front of the window where it wouldn't suck out. We also (took) the fabric covered elevators, ailerons and (the) rudder, and we put metal (covering on them). During our speed tests, they used to tear the fabric off.

Q: Was a four-bladed propeller from a P-63 installed on Cobra II?

A: Yes.

Q: Was that due to the higher torque of its more powerful Allison engine?

A: We had the big engine, and we souped it up. We had water-alcohol injection. We were able to go instead of the standard 59 to 60 inches of manifold pressure, we used to get 75 inches on takeoff by injecting water-alcohol. We needed that big pull by that (P-63) prop to take that torque. (The four-bladed prop was) a lot better for flying, too. It gave us a lot more speed.

Q: Was more right rudder required to hold Cobra II *straight on takeoff because of the higher torque?*

A: I believe it was the opposite, left rudder, because to make it turn in the pylons which was left, the reports from Tex Johnston and Jack Woolams (said) it took 15 to 55 pounds of pressure to hold that rudder in. When you had full throttle with that torque, you had a lot of pressure on the left rudder.

Q: How many flying hours did Tex Johnston have in Cobra II *before he flew it in the Thompson Trophy Race?*

A: We ran tests on the engine. We had the airplane on ground run. We ran tests on the engines to set the alcohol and make sure it was smooth. (We) stored the extra parts. (We) machined .003 inches off the pistons to keep them from freezing up. Then we ran eight to ten hours in the test cell. Then in our flight testing, Tex flew the first flight and tore the elevators. Then he put in about twelve hours flying.

Q: Was Cobra II *difficult to fly?*

A: No, Tex was right at home and so was Jack. To let you know another thing, on the P-39 in the Cleveland Air Race, there used to be an electrical landing gear. It took eight to twelve seconds for the landing gear to come up. We changed the motor on the landing gear. We put a 12-volt motor in a 24-volt system. We got that landing gear up in 4½ seconds! *Cobra II* was off the ground and around the pylons before most were off!

Q: Were any problems noted while flying the race?

A: No. When Tex was around the pylons, he was pulling 70 some inches of manifold pressure. Then he throttled back, and I don't think he pulled more than 62 inches. He saved it. He didn't have to worry about running 75 inches all the time. He pulled back to 59 inches, 60 (or) 61. He was told it was full power from the engine, but we didn't have to go to the extra power.

Q: After the 1946 race, did Mr. Bell restrict his test pilots from future racing?

A: We got in a predicament. Jack Woolams was our chief test pilot, (and) he got killed at the time Bell was into the rocket (plane), the X-1. Slick Goodlin, Tex Johnston and Jack Woolams were the pilots. They (had) worked together for years, and they were real close. Slick Goodlin had a handshake (agreement) with Tex Johnston about flying the X-1, and (they) would give each other's word. But after Woolams got killed, Larry Bell didn't want Tex to fly the airplane (*Cobra II*), but didn't talk Tex out of it. Tex flew in the Cleveland Air Race. After he flew, they settled down. Then they made Tex Johnston the chief test pilot. The X-1 was coming and had to be flown. Tex (and) Jack flew the X-1 as well as Slick. There's a bunch (who) flew it in the drop tests. That's when Slick started asking (because) he thought they should give him more money. Tex Johnston said he'd fly the airplane (instead), (but) Larry Bell said, "No, we lost one chief pilot, I don't want to lose another." That's when he (Larry Bell) turned (the X-1) over to the military. Yes, he (Bell) was concerned. He didn't want his test pilots in any more fancy stuff.

Q: When were you last involved with the P-39?

A: After the Cleveland Air Race, I went back (to Bell Aircraft), (but) the (requirement from the) war was changed. We weren't in (fighter plane) production any more, and I got in the helicopter division. Then in 1947, the Stewart (Rollins) outfit from Indianapolis bought *Cobra II* and (entered) it in the Cleveland Air Race in 1947. I went to the race and helped on the airplane, and we took second (actually, third) that year. That's when Jay Demming couldn't hold the airplane into the pylon because his left leg was giving out. After that, I got out of the P-39s and into the helicopter business, and started taking the helicopters around. I got in with the P-39 at different times, here and there. The Confederate Air Force in Texas—that was years ago—bought a couple of P-39s that were scrapped. I got manuals and some things, and went to Harlingen (Texas) and helped them. We had a 50-year anniversary in April 1989, the 50th anniversary of the P-39's (first) flight, and we were down for that. They had one P-39 from the Confederate Air Force in San Marcos, Texas where it was hangared. They put on an air show (with) their P-39 (for) the 50th anniversary last year.

Q: What is that airplane's condition?

A: It's beautiful! I wish I could find two more! Tex Johnston is looking for one, and I know another guy looking for one.

Q: Have you seen the P-39 at the Kalamazoo Air Museum?

A: No, I didn't.

Q: Did you crew the Confederate Air Force's P-39 after it was restored?

A: No. All I did was help. I had given them parts. That (one) was too far away to do any work, but on weekends I'd go down and look it over, but no work.

Q: Could you compare the P-39 with other fighters of its era?

A: The P-39 was a real good, slick looking airplane. It was an ideal airplane for ground-strafing. I think it was well designed and ahead of its time.

Thank you, Mr. Lajudice.

Mrs. Betty Haas Pfister

World War Two WASP Pilot

Mrs. Pfister was the former civilian owner of the P-39 *Galloping Gertie*, the Smithsonian Institution's Airacobra, now at Silver Hill, Maryland, where the National Air and Space Museum restores its aircraft.

Betty Pfister with *Galloping Gertie*, late 1940s. COURTESY OF THE EAA MUSEUM

Q: Mrs. Pfister, please review your background and when you received your wings?

A: I started flying in 1941. I was at Bennington College in Vermont and had something like 150 hours. Jacqueline Cochran was putting the WASP (Women's Airforce Service Pilot) program together. Through the CAA (Civil Aviation Administration) in Washington, she had records of everyone with a pilot's license, so she sent a telegram to every woman pilot. (She) asked if we would be interested in becoming a member of the WASP program which was the same training program the (Army) Air Force cadets were doing. Most shot back answers in the affirmative. We were extremely interested. I got into the WASPs in February 1943, and I graduated in September 1943. I was first based in the Ferry Command at New Castle Army Air Base, Wilmington, Delaware, and I ferried planes. Then I was transferred to Palm Springs, California, (which was) also a Ferry Command base, (and I) flew single-engine, twin-engine and four-engine bombers. Then my last assignment, the last few months I was in the WASPs, was in the Training Command at Williams Field, in Chandler, Arizona. I was doing test pilot work on advanced trainers known as (North American) AT-6s (Texans).

Q: Did you fly the B-17 and the B-24 (bombers)?

A: I did ferry quite a few of those.

Q: Did you ferry any fighter planes?

A: No. I was on the list. My orders had been cut to go to pursuit school in Brownsville, Texas. I was in the last class of WASPs that would attend, (but) the night before I came down with the measles! I had spots all over, age 21 and really wanted to go to pursuit school more than anything in the world. Instead I was in the infirmary for a week to ten days, and could not go in a later class because there were no later classes. That was one of my real regrets when the WASPs were disbanded in December 1944. The entire WASP program was finished, and I never had flown pursuits. The closest I came was an advanced trainer, the AT-6. I had always wanted to fly a P-38, P-39 (or) P-51. That was my dream. Instead I was having a pretty good time clomping around with bombers, but I definitely loved the idea of flying a fighter. Then I bought a couple of T-6s with a friend of mine, Gloria Heath, another ex-WASP. We had five altogether. We would fix and sell them. We would put a civilian license on them and sell them and make a small profit, just enough to keep flying one for fun. Then one day I saw the P-39 at my home field. I found out who the owner was. He had bought it a couple of weeks before at the Cleveland Air Races. (He) terrified himself flying from Cleveland to New York, and it was for sale.

Q: Was this during the fall of 1946?

A: Yes. I don't have my logbooks handy. I'd have to look at logbooks to give you any good facts, but that's probably close.

Q: I have photostat pages of your logbook which state you purchased Galloping Gertie *on October 31, 1946?*

A: If that's what's in the log, I'm sure it's correct. My memory sure isn't that good!

Q: Records indicate there were two different people, Earl Ortman and a Mr. Mighton, that owned the P-39 before you . . .

A: There was also a guy named Charlie Bing. I think Charlie owned it. I bought the P-39 from Mr. A. C. Vanden-Bulcke.

Q: Where did you first see Galloping Gertie*?*

A: West Chester County Airport in White Plains, New York.

Q: Were you living nearby?

A: Yes. I lived in Scarsdale, New York.

Q: Did you fly Gertie *before you bought her?*

A: That is one of my funny recollections. I remember going to this gentleman and telling him I would like to fly his airplane! He seemed interested in the possibility. I told him I was an ex-WASP. He wanted to know how much P-39 time I had, and I said "none." (He said) well, "the closest thing is a P-38," and (I said), "no, I had never flown one." Then I told him the nearest thing I had (flown) probably was the AT-6, which was *quite* different. I guess I had 600 to 700 hours, a fair amount of T-6 time, but that was not quite like a fighter. We had a small meeting, and he priced the plane. He paid $750 for her, but he ferried it from Cleveland to New York. He wanted to make a slight profit and pay for his fuel, so he priced it at $1,000. He insisted I give him a certified or cashier's check for $1,000 in case I banged up his airplane. I said, "I'm really not sure I want to pay you in case I don't like the plane." I said, "I think I will love it, but just in case I don't like it, I want to give you a check that's refundable in some way". He said, "Well, you could pay me at the rate of $40 an hour for your flying time if you fly it and come back and land it successfully and have no problems." That seemed like a very fair deal to both of us! That's exactly what we did. I came in and landed, and I just told him to keep the $1,000!

Q: Did it still have race number 12?

A: That's correct.

Q: Was it nicknamed JUBA?

A: Yes. That stood for Charlie Bing's two daughters, Judith and Barbara.

Q: What was your name, Galloping Gertie, *based upon?*

A: It was *JUBA* when I bought it. I'm almost sure I named it *Galloping Gertie.* There was a P-51 that raced called *The Galloping Ghost.* I thought that was a neat name, (so) I just called (my P-39) *Galloping Gertie.*

(*The Galloping Ghost*, civilian serial number NX7911, was a P-51D Mustang raced in the Thompson Trophy races from 1946 to 1949. Race number 77 was owned by Bruce Raymond and Steve Beville. It was named after football hero Red Grange. It was little modified but highly polished, and flown flat out at all four air races. It placed second in 1948 whereas in the other three races, it consistently placed fourth.)

Q: Did you fly your P-39 for almost four years?

A: Yes, it was almost four years before I flew it to Niagara Falls to the Bell plant. I was a stewardess with Pan Am, and I was in the middle of a transfer from New York to San Francisco. They were hollering at me to get to San Francisco because they needed us there. Joe Cannon from Bell made the last flight from Niagara to the O'Hare Field storage depot in Chicago. It sat outside the Smithsonian for many years. It was deteriorating terribly. Then the EAA (Experimental Aircraft Association) got interested, and I think they saved that aircraft.

Another shot of Mrs. Betty Haas Pfister with *Galloping Gertie*, her P-39Q, late 1940s. COURTESY MRS. BETTY HAAS PFISTER

They had a guy who had been a P-39 mechanic who was anxious to have one to restore. (This was Ralph Winkel, the crewchief on *Snooks 2nd*, the P-39Q now on display in Buffalo, New York.) Maybe a couple of people in that category. The EAA made an arrangement with the Smithsonian (so) they could do at least cosmetic (repairs). I think it's sitting at Silver Hill (Maryland—the National Air and Space Museum's restoration site), still awaiting an in-depth (restoration).

Q: It is stored inside in a building. They allow tour visitors to see Galloping Gertie.

A: Yes, I did that five years ago. I was very disappointed because they had (painted over) my beautiful paint job. It was lovely. Norman Rockwell had designed the paint job. It was a red and white, my racing paint colors. I thought it was extremely pretty. They put it into olive drab with the Air Force star, (but) it didn't look too good. When they had it at the EAA (Museum) on display at Hales Corner, (I spoke to) a man named Jim Cox who was the head of that museum. I remember telling him I would be happy to pay for putting it in (my) racing colors. I thought we had enough photographs (to) do it easily. Somehow it's not a true military exhibit because you can't put the armament in it. I'm not sure that that particular aircraft ever flew in military service.

Q: I confirmed it was in a Replacement Training Unit at Hamilton Field, California. It also served at Moses Lake and Paine Field before going to McChord Field in Washington. Several weeks ago I interviewed Joe Cannon who was a test pilot with Bell Aircraft . . .

A: Joe Cannon made the last flight from Niagara Falls. Where did he take it then, to Washington?

Q: He flew it to O'Hare (International Airport) in Chicago to a storage facility for the Smithsonian.

A: I have some scrapbooks. I have a picture of Joe Cannon and myself standing on the wing the day I delivered (the P-39) to Niagara Falls. I had another plane, a Navion, that I wanted to move to California when Pan Am transferred me, and I didn't have time to get the P-39 to Chicago, take a commercial (airliner) to New York, pick up the Navion and a friend of mine, and go to San Francisco. They were screaming at me. I was flying to Hong Kong two days later. I'd better get moving!

Q: What did you think of your P-39?

A: I loved it! Of the aircraft I've owned in my life—not all that many, about a dozen or so—the two that outstandingly were at the top of the list (were) number one, the P-39, and second, my Bell helicopter.

Q: Did you compete with your P-39?

A: Yes, I did in some of the air races.

Q: Did Galloping Gertie *win very often?*

A: No; it didn't do very well. One was a cross-country race. It started in West Chester County (New York) and went to Miami (Florida). It flew several times in the Miami Air Races. They did not allow women (pilots) just as they did not in the Sohio (Trophy Race). They were, however, allowed in the Thompson Trophy Race (which was) more of a cross country race than a pylon race. I know Jacqueline Cochran flew that many times. But in the pylon racing for a while in the fighter class, or Unlimited as it's called now, no women were allowed. I think they may now. There's a lady named Sue Parrish who has a P-40 today, but I'm not sure if she flies at Reno.

Q: She and her husband own a flyable P-39Q at the Kalamazoo Air Museum. Is she the lady you are speaking of?

A: Yes, I'm sure she is.

Q: Did you use several engines in your P-39?

A: Yes! I blew up several. The idea was racing, that you fly with wide open throttle. I don't believe in racing for a nice Sunday ride. If you're going to race, you might as well try to win. Everybody else would be flying wide open, so I would too! I still remember my pencilled comments on (my P-39's) instrument panel. I don't know if they're still there, but they were when I saw (the P-39) at Silver Hill. One said "N.E. 60 inches," and underneath I had written, "N.E.U.A.C. 75 inches." That's inches of manifold pressure, but the "N.E." was "never exceed," and the other was "never exceed under any circumstances!" They had not painted over that, even though they had painted fresh black (paint) over the panel because they were curious what it meant! I (also) had a rabbit's foot wired under the seat I put a great deal of faith in!

Q: How many flying hours do you have in your P-39?

A: I'd have to look in the log book. I would say somewhere between 400 and 600 hours, (but) I think closer to 600.

Q: Why did you loan and later donate your P-39 to the Smithsonian?

A: I got married. I had another little plane, a Navion, and I was moving to Aspen, Colorado. It was getting extremely expensive to operate, and I wasn't flying many more races. The time had come. I didn't want to sell it to somebody who would perhaps hurt themselves in it, and I felt I wanted it in a museum. The Air Force Museum (at) Wright Field wanted it, and (so did) the Smithsonian. I put feelers out and got a solid "yes" from everybody. If I had known the Smithsonian was short on space and (the P-39) was to sit outside and have the surfaces deteriorate, I might have felt differently. I was upset when it sat outside for so long, but there was nothing they could do. I was very happy when the EAA moved it.

Q: Have you been advised of the internal condition of the P-39?

A: I haven't. They pickeled the engine when it went in storage. I have no idea. I went to Walter Male who was the curator at the Smithsonian maybe eight to ten years ago. Do you remember the movie "Tora, Tora, Tora" (about the Japanese attack on Pearl Harbor)? I visited him shortly after that movie came out. A friend of mine had flown P-47s for a long time. (He) had been a test pilot at Republic and then hadn't flown much for thirty years. (He) got to go "around the patch" again, and told me what fun it was. I thought I could get my P-39 out! I went to Mr. Male who was the head of the Air and Space Museum. I had an interview and asked (that) if I paid for the insurance and associated costs, could I have the airplane for a week and fly it again? I guess my timing was awful. Unbeknown to me, the Smithsonian had loaned, I think this story is correct, their only Japanese Zero, the only bona fide one, to (the movie studio). During the filming, the (Zero) caught fire and the pilot bailed out, but the "exhibit," as the Smithsonian called it, was lost forever. They said, "Now, what would you do if your airplane caught fire, Mrs. Pfister?" I said, "I would bail out!" "And then we wouldn't have a P-39 anymore," (they replied). They did not let me have the plane back. It was a donation. After a while, it became obvious there was no way I was going to fly it, and if it made them happy to make it a donation, I might as well.

Q: If your P-39 could be rolled out and gone over, would you fly it if you had the chance?

A: Yes, if I had the chance. In two seconds! In a heartbeat!

Q: Have you seen the Confederate Air Force's P-39?

A: No, I never have.

Q: During the P-39's anniversary celebration a year ago, Chuck Yeager flew their P-39.

A: He flew mine once in an air show in Philadelphia! I was flying a two- or three-day show. It was the first time I met Chuck. He really liked P-39s. Chuck flew this one air show. I had been flying with a friend, the same friend I had the AT-6s (with), Gloria Heath. Gloria was in her AT-6 and I would fly *Galloping Gertie.* We would do a mock dogfight. I never did anything terribly earth shattering, maybe a few rolls, but nothing too exciting. One day Chuck asked me if he could fly in my place the following day, and I said sure! We intended to get him a black wig and a blue shirt that would look more like me when he taxied by, but we never had time to get all that! He flew a magnificent show! (He) did about eight snaprolls on takeoff (while) I'm holding my breath! The announcer went crazy! He said, "I've never seen a woman fly like that before. Look at Betty go!" and I'm sitting on the grass watching this! It was exciting! We pretended my aircraft had radio failure. Gloria did all the transmission so there was no voice problem! He flew the act which was twenty minutes, and then he landed. Then I thought maybe that wasn't a smart thing to do and they might be upset seeing ten times a better show than they would have with me flying, and I began to worry about the ethics (since) they were paying me to fly every day, even though I'm giving them a better show with the substitution without telling anyone. I went running to the airplane. Just as I got there, here came this big red convertible with these generals sitting in it to congratulate me on this marvelous flying! Chuck barely got out of the parachute and got it halfway on me, and I had been running so I looked as though I had been doing the flying! They put me in the car and drove to the ramp, and they made (Chuck), he was a captain or a major, walk back! Neither of us said a word! We were afraid of getting in trouble! It's in his book. (See *Yeager, An Autobiography,* by General Chuck Yeager and Leo Janos, page 88, the middle two paragraphs where General Yeager describes this event!)

Q: You mentioned Norman Rockwell designed the color scheme for your P-39?

A: Right.

Q: How did that happen?

A: He was a very close friend of my family.

Q: Was that something you asked him?

A: Yes, I'm sure I asked him.

Q: Did you fly other fighters in addition to your P-39?

A: I flew Woody Edmundson's P-51. He gave me the engine that's in (the P-39) today.

(Woody Edmundson raced a nearly stock P-51D Mustang in the 1946 Thompson Trophy Race, N13Y, race number 45, and took 7th place. He returned in a different Mustang in 1947, an early P-51A that crash-landed on Lap 11 when its engine exploded during the Thompson. Woody survived with bruises and cuts. In 1948, he returned with the same P-51A and same race number 15, but went out of the race on Lap 14 due to engine problems. He did not compete in the last year of the Thompson in 1949.)

He has a plane in the Smithsonian, "Little Butch," a clipped wing monocoupe. He did a lot of aerobatic flying.

Q: Do you have any other comments about your P-39?

A: I thought it was a marvelous plane! I had so much fun; I can't tell you. I had a wonderful time! I had some exciting experiences, especially blowing up the engine a couple of times! We stopped traffic at Jacksonville, Florida, once when I lost an engine coming home from the Miami Air Races. Having flown on full power, sometimes (the engines) wouldn't (last very long). I remember one Miami Air Race, a guy named Johnson was flying. Not Tex Johnston, another Johnson. He went by the last pylon deadstick (the engine was not running) and managed to barely set it down on the runway. They said they wouldn't give him third place because you're supposed to have your engine running! That was never part of any rules we could find.

(Anson Johnson was an airline pilot who raced in the Thompson Trophy Race for several years in the same P-51D Mustang. In the 1947 Thompson, he tried to race N13Y, which had been raced to 7th place in the 1946 Thompson by Woody Edmundson. The engine, however, developed problems, and the Mustang, race number 45, dropped out before the race. The next year was Anson's best showing. Race number 45 took first place in the 1948 Thompson when *Cobra II* vapor locked and the two racing Corsairs developed engine cooling problems. The last year of the Thompson, 1949, saw N13Y, however, not compete due to engine problems. Anson attempted breaking the land plane speed record in June 1952 in this same Mustang, but N13Y couldn't complete the speed runs needed due to engine problems.)

The next time we raced in Miami, I was ferrying (my P-39) to New York and the engine blew up out of Jacksonville. I was at 5,000 to 7,000 feet and the engine disintegrated. The exhaust stacks were blowing off behind me. It was hard to keep my feet on the rudder pedals (because) it was vibrating so badly. I called Jacksonville. It was the only time I declared an emergency. I said I would like the first possible runway, and they cleared Eastern, American Airlines and everything you could think of out of my way! I popped the gear down when the runway was in sight. (I) got it down all right, but that engine was just finished. I had bits of pistons and rings floating around. Then it sat until Woody gave me that new engine.

Thank you, Mrs. Pfister.

Colonel Virgil E. "Sandy" Sansing

Retired United States Air Force Colonel

Sandy Sansing is one of the two current pilots for the Confederate Air Force's P-39 along with Colonel Bob Ayers. He began flying with the Army Air Corps in November 1941 and retired in 1973. During those many years as a fighter pilot, he flew the P-40, the P-47 and the P-51. He shot down one German Bf-109 in Europe while once being shot down over France and escaping to England. In 1952, he was a Squadron Commander and a Group Commander flying F-84s over Korea. He had 350 forward air controller missions over Vietnam during 1966 and 1967. Colonel Sansing joined the CAF in 1975. In addition to flying the Airacobra regularly, he is a check pilot for the CAF's A-26, TBM and P-38. In 1981, he became the project officer in charge of rebuilding the Cen-Tex Wing's P-38, "Scatterbrain Kid II," whose restoration was underwritten by Colonel John Stokes of the CAF. Colonel Stokes is today the sole sponsor of the CAF's P-39.

Q: Colonel Sansing, what was your prior flying experience?

A: I spent 31 years in the Air Force flying mostly fighters, although I did not fly the P-39 until I joined the Confederate Air Force.

Q: What aircraft did you fly?

A: I started with the P-40, then the P-47, P-51, F-80, F-84, F-86, F-104 and lots of other different ones, (such as the) A-26 (and the) C-47.

Q: What were your total military hours before retirement?

A: I had 7,000 hours. I've put in over 5,000 more since I retired. A little over 12,000 hours (total) flying time.

Q: How many hours do you have flying the Confederate Air Force's P-39?

A: About 300.

Q: When did you first fly it?

A: Five years ago.

Q: What do you think of it?

A: It's a fine airplane. It's fun to fly. You hear bad stories about it, but none have been confirmed. I found the '39 (to be) like most aircraft. If you fly within the (performance) envelope they were designed, you won't get into trouble. But if you do things they're not built to do, then, yes, you'll get in trouble.

Q: Is the Confederate Air Force's P-39 painted in Russian markings?

Colonel Sansing at the CAF's 50th anniversary celebration in San Marcos, Texas, on April 8, 1989. COURTESY BELL HELICOPTER/TEXTRON

A: Yes.

Q: Is it painted after any particular pilot's airplane, or is it a general color scheme?

A: At the time (this) plane was rebuilt, the Confederate Air Force had (another) P-39 in U.S. markings. The Confederate Air Force (also) had a P-63 in French markings, so the decision was to put this '39 in Russian markings.

Q: That other P-39 is now with the Kalamazoo Air Museum?

A: Yes.

Q: Did you fly that P-39?

A: No, I did not.

Q: Is your P-39 assigned to a wing of the Confederate Air Force?

A: Yes, to the Central Texas Wing.

Q: Is the P-39 the only airplane that wing is responsible for?

A: No. We are rebuilding a P-38 which is about ready to fly. We maintain a replica of a "Kate," a Japanese torpedo bomber, and then a UC-78 (transport).

Q: Has all the military hardware, such as armor and armament, been deleted from your P-39?

A: Well, it's ornamental. It's not real armament.

Q: Has a water spray system been added to your P-39's intake to reduce overheating on the ground?

A: The radiator on the '39 is not sufficient to cool the airplane if you stay on the ground a while. We put a spray bar in front of the radiator and a water tank in the nose where the ammunition cans used to go, and (we) put a pump in. If we stay on the ground and it starts getting warm, we just spray water on the radiator to cool it. That's the only time you need it.

Q: How would you characterize the airplane's handling?

A: It's a good flying airplane and fun to fly. It got passed by technological advancements. It doesn't have the performance of the P-51 and the P-38, but during its day, it was an outstanding airplane. It still is as far as flying goes.

Q: Is the P-39's current engine identical to the original, or is it an upgraded Allison?

A: It's a V-1710-85.

Q: Is it a replacement or was it in the plane when rebuilt?

A: The engine in it we changed two years ago. It was a new military engine that had never been in an airplane.

Q: Is your P-39 in stock condition, or does it have modifications?

A: We have a current radio. We had to give up the old military radio a long time ago because there were no parts nor anyone to work on (it). (Also) the artificial horizon is a civilian model. Nobody wants to fool with the old military version anymore. But for major modifications, there are none.

Q: Was your P-39 bought by Colonel John Stokes who still maintains the airplane?

A: That is correct. He has backed the Confederate Air Force for many years and has helped them. He purchased the P-39 and donated it to them, and he has been maintaining it for them ever since. He had a Focke-Wulf 44, a German biplane trainer. He maintained that for quite a few years and finally donated that to the Confederate Air Force. They have that at Harlingen (Texas, the Confederate Air Force's headquarters) now.

Q: Is he the sole support of this airplane?

A: Yes. At one time he owned 34 warbirds. It was not unusual to see 12 to 14 of his airplanes at a Confederate Air Force show. He's gotten out of the business. The only thing he's got personally is an A-26 (an American twin-engine World War Two bomber).

Q: Is your P-39 based at San Marcos, Texas?

A: Yes.

Q: Is that a private airport?

A: No, it's a municipal airport. John Stokes had a hangar there. He was keeping (the P-39) in the hangar at San Marcos.

Q: Is the airplane limited to specific numbers of hours or displays it is allowed to fly annually?

A: No.

Q: I know the British Battle of Britain Memorial Flight's restored planes (mostly Spitfires and Hurricanes) are limited and rotated frequently so that a specific number of flying hours are not exceeded each year.

A: It varies (with us) from year to year. It depends who is putting the show on and what kind of show they are putting on.

Q: Is there a specific mechanic assigned to your P-39?

A: We have two mechanics who are full-time employees. They are taking care of the '39 and do most of the work on the Kate, but they are employees of John Stokes.

Q: Do the mechanics for the P-39 have prior experience, or is that something they had adapted to?

A: Not particularly on the P-39, but both are retired Air Force mechanics. They have a lot of experience on World War Two aircraft.

Q: Have you flown at air shows and had visitors who flew the P-39 exchange stories?

A: Yes.

Q: Do they go into detail?

A: Not too much because the '39 wasn't used too

much. The P-40 and P-39 were the only things we had when the war started, but they (the Air Force) replaced them with the '47s, the '51s and the '38s as quickly as they could. The '39 was used in the South Pacific and North Africa, but they replaced them quickly. Most people I've talked to had limited time in the P-39. They still go by the old story that the P-39 was a "killer" when it wasn't. The people that flew it quite a bit liked the airplane. The Russians loved it.

Q: Of the different stories about the P-39's bad habits, have you experienced any flying the Confederate Air Force's Airacobra?

A: No. One story was that the airplane would "tumble." During the war, Bell Aircraft offered any pilot that could show them a tumble with the airplane $5,000 on the spot! Nobody ever did it.

Q: Was Chuck Yeager invited to fly your P-39 at an air show within the past few years?

A: Yes. We took (the P-39) to Las Vegas, Nevada for the "Gathering of Eagles." He flew it there.

Q: Did he like it?

A: The first fighter he flew was a P-39. He thinks a lot of the airplane, and that's the first '39 he's flown since. As far as I know, yes, he did enjoy it!

Q: Are there plans to add another P-39 to the Confederate Air Force?

A: Not to the Confederate Air Force. A fellow named Tallichet—he's out in California—was having two rebuilt. Whether he's going to fly or use them as static displays, I really don't know.

Q: Colonel Sansing, do you have any final comments about the P-39?

A: I think it's a great airplane. I've enjoyed flying it, and hopefully I'll fly it for a few more years. I think the Confederate Air Force is doing a great job keeping these old things going.

Q: Do you have parts problems?

A: Not a lot. We have been fortunate. Most of the parts we had to replace we (found) parts for. There's a couple we had to manufacture.

Q: Does the Confederate Air Force maintain its own facilities?

A: No. You go (to) a good machine shop with a good machinist and a metallurgist and show what you've got (so) they can copy it.

Q: What would you estimate is the lifespan of your P-39?

A: As long as they take good care of the airplane, it's going to keep flying. This airplane has 800 hours on it which is not much. It's good for a long time if properly maintained.

Thank you, Colonel Sansing.

Colonel Paul Bechtel

World War Two Fighter Pilot

Colonel Paul Bechtel, July 1990. COURTESY COLONEL BECHTEL

As a World War Two Fighter Pilot, Colonel Bechtel had five confirmed victories, two of which were while flying P-39s.

Q: Colonel Bechtel, when did you join the service and when did you receive your wings?

A: I entered flying school after I graduated college in June 1939. Our class graduated Kelly Field at San Antonio (Texas) on the 23rd of March, 1940. Fifty were sent to Selfridge Field, Michigan six (to) eight weeks after we graduated flying school. We joined two Pursuit Groups, that's what they called fighters in those days, the 1st Pursuit Group and the 31st Pursuit Group. The first guy in the alphabet went to the 1st Group, the second one to the 31st, the third to the 1st, and so on. I ended in the 31st. We were taught to fly P-35s which was the Seversky (the forerunner of Republic Aircraft) airplane. We learned to fly (Curtiss) P-36s (the P-40's predecessor), but we didn't have any in the 31st Group. We had to chisel them off the 1st Group!

Q: When did you arrive in Selfridge, Michigan?

A: Around the first of May, 1940.

Q: When did the P-39s arrive?

A: March or April 1941.

Q: Were these P-39Cs?

A: No. These would probably be As, if there was such an airplane. I don't know which went into production first. (Note: The P-39C was the first production Airacobra). They might have arrived earlier, like late January or early February. (Flight records show P-39s at Selfridge in January and February.)

Q: You earlier discussed your involvement in the YP-39 program. Were you with the YP-39s before the Airacobras came to Selfridge? Where did you fly the YP-39s?

A: I'm sure (the YP) preceded the production models we were getting. There were two or three (YP-39s). They had been sent to Patterson Field near Dayton, Ohio, which is now part of Wright-Patterson Air Force Base. Patterson was a depot but involved with Wright Field where the testing was. Service tests were conducted on the YP (-39), the pre-production model. There was an XP. Following that were the service test models which were called YPs. Following that were the P-39s with some other number (and/or letter).

Q: Were you on temporary duty at Patterson Field to fly the YP-39s?

A: Yes. We were sent for two weeks. I was there twice. I remember that well because I had been married the 15th of February, and about three weeks after, I got sent for two weeks temporary duty at Patterson. I didn't like it, but it worked out!

Q: Were the YP-39s the first P-39s you flew?

A: No. I might have flown the others (P-39Cs) before. (Flight records indicate a YP-39 was at Selfridge in January or February.)

Q: What was your assignment with the YPs?

A: It was a service test. They wanted time on the engine and the airplane. They had general schedules. We would see how fast we could climb. We went to altitudes that were possible which would have been around 25,000 or 30,000 feet. (We were) limited by the oxygen masks. That's something that was new because we had been sucking the old pipe stems on the end of a tube with the P-35!

Q: How many hours did you fly the YPs during those two weeks?

A: Maybe twenty. We flew every day. We would get two hours. That's a five-day week. That was prewar schedules!

Q: Could you compare the YPs with the production P-39s?

A: They (the YPs) were very representative (of the production P-39s). I got one (YP-39) in an inverted spin and rattled my head around the cockpit. The YP had boltheads sticking out (which) they hadn't covered with rubber bumpers, and I banged my head! We were wearing cloth helmets.

Q: Were the YPs armed?

A: I don't think they were. This was too soon, and there was no firing (them). I don't think I fired a P-39 until I got on Christmas Island (overseas).

Q: Were the YPs faster than production Airacobras?

A: No. There wasn't any difference; the same engine, the same body contours. There were no major changes between the YP and the early (P-39s).

Q: Did you see the prototype XP-39?

A: No.

Q: Did you speak with Bell's test pilots while at Patterson?

A: I don't remember. They were (there). We ferried (P-39s) from the plant at Buffalo all over the east coast because we were the first to fly them. We were in and out of Bell's plant for the next year.

Q: Did Bell Aircraft debrief you?

A: I don't remember much debriefing by Bell. They could have been debriefing me and I might not have known it!

Q: What was your P-39 flying experience when you returned to Selfridge, Michigan?

A: I was in the 39th Pursuit Squadron in the 31st Pursuit Group. They decided to outfit the 39th Squadron with P-39s as the first unit in the Air Corps. We flew them quite a bit. This is one reason why we got in the tests and why we were called to ferry (them), because the airplane was not hard to fly. It was the first tricycle (landing) gear I experienced. Once you tried that you found it was wonderful compared to the tail wheel. It didn't ground loop. I thoroughly enjoyed flying it.

Q: What was good about the airplane's performance?

A: I didn't have much to compare it with other than the P-35 and the P-36. It (the P-39) was five or six years newer. A lot of change had taken place. It was faster. I don't know it handled any better in the air. It was certainly more (of a) pleasure to land and taxi because the P-35 was a great ground looper. This airplane (the P-39) had no problem like that. It was a pleasure to fly.

Q: What was the visibility from the airplane?

A: Very good!

Q: What about rearward?

A: It was as good as anything I flew. I flew the P-40, the P-38, the F4U (Corsair) and the F-6F (Hellcat) in combat.

Q: What was negative about the P-39?

A: Until I got into combat, it was all up! When I got into combat, I found it was not the greatest airplane to fight a war with! We didn't have *any* airplanes in the American forces that could maneuver with the Japanese Zero. We found this quickly. The things I found about the P-39 I didn't care for in combat were, first, the guns. The (other) people who had four or six .50 calibre (machine guns) could do more damage when they hit an airplane than we could with the P-39 where we had four free firing .30 calibre (machine guns) and two .50 calibres (firing) through the prop, and then we had that 37mm (cannon) which turned out to be a complete loss. I never got over three shots before it jammed. We swapped them (the 37mm cannons) as fast as we could for 20mm guns (cannons) because those fired fine and we liked them. The first we ran into them (the 20mm cannons) was with the British P-400s. They were equipped with the 20mm (cannon), and every one we could salvage, we put in the P-39.

Q: Where were you based during combat with the P-39?

A: My squadron was sent to Christmas Island which was 1200 miles south of Honolulu, (Hawaii. It is just north of the equator in the Pacific Ocean) in late January 1942. We acquired our allotment of 25 P-39s a month later. They came in huge crates. That's another story about getting those off ship and onto a lighter, and off a lighter and onto the shore, and haul them 18 miles to an airport, take them out of the crates and build them! They came in crates that were 40 feet long; 8 feet high, maybe 9; and 7 feet wide. The crates weighed 14,000 pounds (with) one airplane inside. We expected new airplanes. We were a little brokenhearted when we opened the boxes and found airplanes that had mud from the Carolina Maneuvers the previous summer and fall! These were the airplanes we were given to fight a war! We moved in late fall 1942 from Christmas (Island) to the New Hebrides (mid-way between Christmas Island and Australia). I took eleven pilots to Guadalcanal in middle December. We relieved other people fighting there in P-400s and P-39s. We took a tour of combat to the first of February (1943). Then we went on rest leave to New Zealand. This was the first we had flown airplanes in combat. None had aerial gunnery. We didn't have any way to get it. We didn't tow targets. Nobody in our squadron thought up shooting at shadows yet. So, air-to-ground, we had a lot of practice, but as far as air-to-air, we hadn't any, and it showed! You just don't do well when you don't have adequate training.

Q: Do you have two kills flying the P-39?

A: Yes. The first combat I got was over Munda (in the center of the Solomon Islands, east of Papua New Guinea) on Christmas Eve 1942. We were providing cover for (Douglas) (Navy) SBDs (dive bombers) dive bombing Munda. Munda had been operational less than a week as far as the Japanese were concerned. We caught a flock of (Japanese) airplanes taking off. I say "we"; the Marines in their F4Fs shot down a bunch in the traffic (landing and takeoff) pattern. We ran into (the Zeros) around 15,000 or 16,000 (feet). They thought we were other Zeros and let us join on their tail, which was very accommodating! I shot down one. (I) was working on another when they discovered we were there. After that, things went to pot! We scattered all over the place. When I (realized it), I had one on my tail, (but) I evaded him (when) I spun it, and it worked! It wasn't intentional. When I came out of the spin, I didn't see my friends. Then I located another single airplane over Munda. I went to join. As I got closer, I found he was another Zero, but again he was accommodating like the others and let me join on his tail! This time I knew how much lead to put on (my machine gun fire), and I got him, too!

Q: When you shot the first one down, was that with machine gun or cannon fire?

A: I never fired the cannon. All I was shooting were machine guns.

Q: Was that the .30s and the .50s?

A: Yes.

Q: When you encountered the second Zero, was that the same method?

A. Right, the .30s and the .50s.

Q. Please compare the P-39's maneuverability with the Zero.

A: We (the United States) didn't have airplanes that could maneuver with the Zero because they (our planes) had heavier wing loading (the ability of the wings to lift the weight of the plane, with American designs having wings usually lifting heavier loads). They (the Zeros) didn't carry any armor plate, and they didn't carry flameproof (fuel) tanks. Their airplanes were lighter. As a result, they were more maneuverable. It made it miserable. The only way you could cope with them (the Zeros) was to hit them and get out until you could turn around and hit them again. This is not a very handy way to fight a war, but it works!

Q: What about straight line acceleration?

A: We could outrun them, particularly going down hill.

Q: Did you have situations where the Zero pilots knew if they got high enough, you couldn't attack them because of the poor high-altitude capability of the P-39?

A: I never had that experience. By the time we got into the high-altitude work, we had swapped to P-38s. We did get into combat with them (the Zeros) up to altitudes better than 30,000 feet. The Zeros could get there, and we could (also) with the P-38s. The P-39 could have gotten there, but it might have been a little sloppy. (With) the P-400s, the guys that went to Guadalcanal (who) had those to fly were in trouble because that was an English (export) airplane. The English used a high-pressure oxygen system. We used a low-pressure, and we had no high-pressure capability. The first (pilots) in Guadalcanal couldn't go much above 10,000 to 12,000 feet because they didn't have oxygen. It isn't smart to get up higher because you run into trouble. Your mind doesn't work as well (in thin air).

Q: Were many P-39s used in ground-support or ground-strafing roles because of their cannon and heavier firepower? Did you fly more ground-support missions?

A: Yes, because of the deficiency of the guns. It became obvious quickly to us and I'm sure to those watching us fly that six .50s (on other fighters) were more destructive than four .30s and two .50s firing through the prop (on the P-39). On the other hand, you could kill or injure as much with a .30 calibre as you could with a .50. The P-39 was good strafing, and there was plenty strafing on Guadalcanal.

Q: Please compare the P-39 with the P-40.

A: The P-40 had a good gun installation. It had six free-firing .50s, a big advantage over the P-39. If you got your guns on somebody (in the P-40) and hit him, you really hurt him. The .30 calibres (in the P-39) didn't seem to do that much. That was the biggest difference. The P-39 was the sweetest airplane I flew, (but) the lousiest airplane I fought a war in! I liked the airplane, but I didn't care for it for fighting. We had the problem of manually charging the guns. The cables to the .30s in each wing were on the floor. To charge the guns, you pulled the cable up high. If you lift something chest high, your pull (strength) is no good. That's the hardest part because you're at the last of the spring compression in the machine guns. The same was true of the .50s. They were manually charged. You reached forward on either side, grabbed the handle and pulled to the rear. As you got to the rear, your pull was (at) a minimum but where you needed it most. I'll never forget flying an F4U and finding the three guns on each side had hydraulic chargers. Hit a button with the palm of your hand on the right side and three guns were charged. Hit another button on the left and (the) three left guns were charged. If you're in the the fight and your guns start jamming, it's handier to hit a button than fly an airplane and act like a spider pulling guns to charge them! These were detrimental (to) the combat capability of the P-39.

Q: Did you encounter "tumbling" in the P-39?

A: I never did, nor any people in my organization.

Q: Was tumbling part of the P-39's reputation?

A: I didn't hear about it until the end of my tour in the Pacific or after I got back to the States.

Q: How many hours did you fly the P-39?

A: I would guess 500 or 600.

Q: Do you think the P-39 fulfilled its mission, considering it was one of our earliest fighters?

A: It fought a good war. It didn't shoot down a lot of airplanes, but it served other purposes very, very well.

Q: Were there any aces scoring all five kills in the P-39?

A: There was one. *Fighter Aces Quarterly Magazine* (has) written up one fellow (who) was in New Guinea as shooting down five airplanes in a P-39. As far as they knew, he was the only guy who became an ace in a P-39.

Q: Could you compare the P-39 with the P-400 as far as equipment and performance?

A: They (the P-400s) weren't different except for the oxygen system and the 20mm cannon. The oxygen system was a shortcoming, (but) the 20mm was better. Other than that, there wasn't any difference. They flew, handled and were maintained the same. They used identical parts.

Q: Was the life of the Allison engine in the P-39 longer than it was in other Allison-powered fighters because the extension shaft absorbed some of the vibration?

A: Not from my knowledge. (The) vibration from that shaft that went between your legs; I never experienced any problems, none whatsoever; nor do I know anybody that did.

Q: Did you find the P-39's vibration would cause your legs additional fatigue?

A: No. I never had complaints, nor did I hear of any. Most everybody liked to fly it. They didn't like to fight in it, for the reasons I mentioned.

Thank you, Colonel Bechtel.

Colonel Charles Falletta

World War Two Fighter Pilot

Colonel Falletta had 16 World War Two aerial victories. The first six were achieved while flying P-39s over New Guinea.

Q: Colonel Falletta, please review when you joined the military and received your wings.

A: I went in the Air Cadet Program in 1940. I graduated Kelly Field in Class 41-D (in) late May or June. From there I went to Mitchel Field, New York to fly P-40s (as) my first assignment.

Q: Where were you introduced to the P-39?

A: At Mitchel Field. When we went to Mitchel, they had P-40s. I believe we were the first squadron in the Air Corps to get the P-39, the 36th Fighter Squadron (actually one of the first). We converted from the P-40 to the P-39 at Mitchel. (It was) one of the easiest airplanes I have converted to because of the tricycle gear. We were having trouble with the P-40s. They (the pilots) were groundlooping because of the low tail wheel. They raised the tail wheel about six inches (on those P-40s), and it got better. We read the Tech Orders (on the P-39), (but) had no instructions. One technical representative (from Bell) talked to us. (He) let us sit in the cockpit (and) gave us what he called the "blindfold test": you reached and found the landing gear handle, the throttle and those things. (Then he) said, "You're on your own!"

Q: Which model P-39 was that?

A: It was one of the earliest. I don't know what number.

Q: When were you were activated for combat?

A: (When) war was declared on December 8, 1941, we were called to base. (We) went on submarine (coastal) patrol with the P-39s at Stratford, Connecticut. Nobody in the squadron had fired the gun (on) the P-39. We had the 37mm cannon. Then we were to fly the airplanes to Dayton, Ohio. They were to prepare (the P-39s) for shipment on (a) boat. We came to Mitchel, got on a train and went to San Francisco, California. This was after December 15th or 20th. On December 7th, we were submarine patrolling at Bridgeport, I think it was, instead of Stratford. We caught a train, went to San Francisco and got on a ship. I believed we were going to Java (an island northwest of Australia, but south of the Philippines), (but) it was a secret then. Something happened; I think the Philippines fell (to the Japanese forces) while we were en route. We ended in Brisbane, Australia (on the east coast) at Amberly Field. The airplanes were assembled by American crewchiefs and Australian mechanics. We picked up pilots in Sydney (Australia, on the southeast coast) doing nothing that were displaced en route to the Philippines. We started training. We trained two weeks, then six officers and I were called to a tent one night at the field. Colonel Freddy Smith asked for volunteers. (He said), "I've got to send six people (to New Guinea) to join the Australian (P-40) squadron." This was the 75th (Royal Australian Air Force) Squadron commanded by Squadron Leader Jackson. I didn't volunteer, but I went! If they're shooting bullets, why, I'm not going there voluntarily! He said, "You're going, so I want *you* to volunteer. This is for the rest!" I was not the top vintage of officers. There were some that had ten to fifteen years service and were Lieutenants and Captains, and I was relatively new in the Air Corps. I had civilian time before the Air Corps. I instructed cadets in PT-19s (a military two-seat training plane) before I became a cadet. I had as much experience as far as flying, but I didn't have the military experience *and* time in service. We took six P-39s, left Brisbane (and) went to Horn Island (the north central tip of Australia) stopping for gas along the route. (We) stopped at Townsville, Rockhampton, Cooktown and Horn Island (all on the northeastern coast of Australia). We flew the channel (the Coral Sea to Papua New Guinea). Bill Meng was the flight leader. He was experienced. When we got to Jackson (Seven Mile) Field in Port Moresby, New Guinea, Bill Meng checked the field for obstacles. He radioed, "everything looks good." I was in landing position; my flaps down, the wheels down; (and) I landed. I (was) the first American pilot to land on New Guinea in the war. We were briefed by the Australians that night. We had crewchiefs, an armament officer and one armor enlisted man. This was the first any of us except Captain Meng were to fire the cannon on that airplane or the other (machine) guns. The next morning, (Squadron Leader) Jackson (met us in the air over New Guinea). They were on another field. We would decide what we would do the next morning. Our mission was to fly with them. They (the Australians) were flying P-40s. It was almost an impossible task. The P-39 was much faster (than the P-40) at lower altitude, (but) not as fast higher. The difference was (that it was) hard to stay with the formation. Our instructions were, "If you can stay with us, come on, we'll go on. If you can't, do whatever you have to." I managed to stay with the squadron commander the first day, and I shot an airplane down in the P-39! I couldn't make the cannon work. I got one shot, but that's all. I never got over one shot, and I flew 144 combat missions in the P-39. The P-39 is a unique airplane. It's put together well. You can dive the living daylights and expect to make it. It's not going apart. That was one of the most outstanding features. One of the weakest was it took too long to the service ceiling which was about 25,000 to 26,000 feet. Above that, you get so mushy it would take several minutes to get a few feet (higher). You're just mushing on up. We couldn't practice (formation flying) at altitude with the P-40s well. We did try every day. I'm not sure how long we were there (in Papua New Guinea), about four to six weeks, maybe shorter. All the time my squadron was there, that little element—it wasn't a squadron; just six airplanes (in New Guinea) to find what it was about; we saw some combat, not a lot. Of the six planes, we managed to keep three (or) four in the air, (but) no more. Of the three or four that got airborne, there was at least one that would come back for various reasons. I managed to fly every mission, every day, sometimes two missions a day, and sometimes three. I (jumped) a Japanese bomber formation once. I happened to be above. It took an hour to climb, but I was just above. I got my nose down to get speed and scattered bullets through the formation (and) broke it up. They didn't get a bombing run. Not one 37mm (shell) popped off that time, (but) the .30 calibre and .50 calibre (machine guns) worked perfectly. I left two or three bombers smoking. I didn't see any go down. You couldn't get credit for airplanes unless you had three sources of information that saw them go down. Of course, I'm by myself (on that attack). I was with the Australian squadron, but they didn't attack. I got no credit for that.

Q: Did you have other confirmed kills with the P-39?

A: I've got several confirmed kills (in the P-39). It would take too long to talk about (the process of) confirmation (of kills). We were the first six (P-39s in New Guinea). We didn't have paper to write history, (and) that part is missing. There is no history of those six weeks. But I've got a Distinguished Service Cross that says I shot one down. I've got a Silver Star that says I shot one or two down, along with other medals. I can only find one order that says an airplane is confirmed. A Japanese man researching history said he had two orders that showed I had two. I don't have all orders. I kept the materials I had, and I had sixteen.

Q: Were all sixteen kills with the P-39?

A: No. I got a few (later) in the P-38, but I say six were in the P-39. We converted to P-38s later in the 80th (Fighter) Squadron, (and) I became the commander. I was also in the Korean conflict.

Q: Please assess the P-39 in combat.

A: The airplane was absolutely excellent at altitudes of 8,000 to 12,000 feet. If you found anybody that low, they (had) better watch out! It was not good at high altitudes. If I was fighting with another airplane that couldn't get higher than me, it might have been comparable. But the Japanese Zero would get (to) 30,000, 31,000, 32,000 feet and maneuver well. We couldn't.

Q: Of the six Japanese airplanes you shot down, were any Zeros?

A: I ran the figure of six. It might have been eight or nine. The first one I shot down was a bomber. The rest were Zeros in the P-39. I got a few more bombers in the P-38 because we could go higher or they were bombing lower.

Q: Was the P-39 comparable at lower altitude with the Zero?

A: If you met a Japanese (plane) at 12,000 feet, he was a dead duck with the P-39.

Q: Were your kills in the P-39 with the machine guns or the cannon?

A: Every one was (with) machine guns. We would normally test our guns on the (combat) approach. We could get one round out of the cannon. You weren't shooting at anybody, you were on the approach, and then (it) would jam. We started to hold and fire it the one time when we were in range. The three or four times I had a good opportunity, the guns jammed before one (37mm shell) came out!

Q: How maneuverable was the P-39 against the Zero?

A: The Zero could make a tighter turn. They could go into a Lufbery (a World War One French Fighter Pilot) circle of a loop and shoot on any approach you tried. You couldn't do that in the P-39. There was a difference in the flying characteristics. The Zero flew like our (advanced) trainer, (the North American Aviation) AT-6. It looked like one. You could maneuver that well, but the Zero had a more powerful engine. They (the Zeros) didn't have armor plating. We were loaded like lead on that P-39! If they had taken that off, it would have done the job, but we believed in saving pilots. (The armor plating) made it hard to get there. That's not the only thing. The supercharger was needed.

Q: Would the P-39 have been different if equipped with a supercharger?

A: Yes! It would have done at 30,000 and 35,000 feet what it would at 10,000 or 12,000 feet. We could have raked them over. They were to put it on once, but changed their mind.

Q: Did you fly the P-39 on strafing missions or ground-support?

A: Innumerable times; many, many times. In Lae, Salamaua, Goodenough Island and those islands (these are eastern Papua New Guinea) the Japanese had airplanes on. Most was Lae (east central coast at the center of the harbor) because that was the position of the (Japanese) aircraft that were giving Port Moresby the biggest headache.

Q: What did you like about the P-39?

A: It was well-built, sturdy, and I had all the confidence in the world in it. I wasn't afraid to fly straight down as hard as I wanted and pull out. (It) didn't bother me. Another good thing was the visibility when you were flying. You could see everywhere. They used to call me "Hawkeye!" I never failed to see the enemy. My head was on a pivot all the time. I liked the P-39. I know a lot of people didn't. They were scared of it. That's why they didn't like it. It isn't an airplane you can mess around with. You have to know what you're doing. Stall it on a steep turn coming in for a landing, and that's it. You won't get out. There's a lot of problems, (but) I wouldn't call them bad.

Q: I heard about the aircraft "tumbling," but nobody I have spoken with has given me a confirmation.

A: I'll give it to you! I tumbled it in combat. I was chasing a Zero straight up. The next thing I knew I was in a position I couldn't get out of. I was falling going over and over. I couldn't get control on my tail (control surfaces). It was loosely turning. The stick; you could spin it. You could put your finger on it and go around and around. There was no control. I was the first in New Guinea that tumbled that got out of it. I lowered my flaps, and the flaps came off. The next thing I did was lower the landing gear. It (the plane) vibrated, turned on its back, and vibrated more. I felt the control stick getting tight when I grabbed it, got out of the tumble and landed.

Q: What gyration was this when tumbling?

A: I could see the earth underneath and the mountains, (but) you couldn't tell. You could tell you were going over in a big slow loop and coming back up in another, and then it would get faster. Sometimes it would slow down. It didn't stay the same speed all the time. It would tumble, but I believe it's almost impossible to get into one. I don't believe I could tumble one (again) if I tried.

Q: This happened during combat?

A: I had my head in the gunsight. I was chasing a Japanese Zero up. He was outclimbing me. (The P-39) went over on its back. (It) went in a side-swirl and then a little easier loop. The loops were not big. They were not like you go over way down and come up. They were little ones.

Q: What other aspects of the P-39 were not favorable?

A: Look! The tumbling effect was not anything bad. You could count on your hands the people that tumbled that airplane. That's no more unusual than any other airplane that's got a little problem. I didn't mean tumbling was that bad. I was never concerned about tumbling, but I did tumble once. I couldn't guarantee it was *the* tumble everyone was talking about. I got into the (worst) position I've been in, and I couldn't get out. I assumed it was a tumble. I could be wrong. It might not have been. I want to be accurate on it.

Q: I have researched your P-39D, Army Air Force Serial Number 41-6951. May I ask about it and what has happened since the war? I know you were involved with its restoration (in Australia—see the surviving P-39s section).

A: The six pilots returned to Australia. We were going (to New Guinea). Our 35th Squadron went; we were the 36th. The day before our squadron was to go, the 35th lost eight to ten airplanes. The first echelon of our squadron got through. I was to bring six of the sick airplanes, the ones out of commission. We got those in commission . . . (and I was soon asked), "Why aren't you taking off?" I said, "Well, the weather doesn't look good, and I can't get weather reports north. I've been there and the weather is dangerous." (I was told), "They need those airplanes. Get airborne." I even said, "This is an order?" and (I was told) "It's an order." We left Townsville (in the P-39s) and then stopped for gas at Cooktown and Horn Island (on Australia's northeast coast). The weather was fair then, but we couldn't get a weather report from Horn Island or Cooktown, so we took off. It was 3:30 in the afternoon. The weather got worse. We passed the no return point, (and) we didn't have enough gas to go back. I put the squadron in a tight formation. We got as low as fifty feet over the water to get to Horn Island. They had no homing devices. None of my pilots could fly instruments well, no more than needle, ball and airspeed. We circled and we talked to Horn Island. I couldn't understand them, (and) they couldn't understand me. We were in a tropical storm. We couldn't do anything. I told everybody to drop their belly tanks. I started a steep circle and had to climb to 150 feet to lead. That's like shaking the stick (control column) to go that high. I (finally) said, "Okay, I see a field. I think we can make it. Drag it slowly. I'm going for a landing. If I make it, all of you come in." I landed (with my) wheels down in the jungle in the only clear area. I took it almost to a stop when my left (main) landing gear cracked off. (My P-39) hit a little stump. (The) number two man (Lieutenant Walt Harvey) came in wheels up. The other four got lost. When you're at 50 to 150 feet with a fighter plane in a strange country in a storm, there is not much leeway. Everybody is shook up. They made a left turn and got back. (They) landed on the beach. (Lieutenant Love) was killed (on his landing). We were trying to get our airplanes to the combat zone following the ones that had gone ahead two days before. (Several years ago), the Australian Broadcasting System wanted to make a film of this incident. They asked me to bring any of my pilots. Everyone survived the war except the one (in the landing accident). The Air Force was to send us "space available," (but) that petered out. The Australian broadcasting company said, "we can't bring all six. We can't afford it for that film." (They) agreed to bring my wife with me. We made this film of the incident. They told me they made the film because some younger

Australians forgot (the war). They were getting anti-American. They had to wake (them) as to who helped win the war. That's why they made (the documentary), so they could show it on a Sunday afternoon.

Q. When did you learn your airplane was being restored?

A: Syd Beck, the fellow who has the airplane, wrote (to) Air Force headquarters that he was to get a P-39 out of the jungle. He gave the plane's number. He said, "I'd like to know who was flying it, if he's still alive, and any history." The Air Force sent the letter to me and said, "It's our policy not to give names and locations of our people. If you're interested, answer his letter." I answered. He invited us, so my wife and I went. (We) stayed a couple weeks, watched them work on the airplane (and) did some sightseeing.

Q: Is it completed?

A: He's had it completed! It will never fly. It sat in the jungle too long. They're not going to redo it to that extent. They put their sheet metal on as the other had rotted. It's a show job. It was in Townsville, Australia, in a hangar. In the last year and a half, he moved to Mareeba (north of Townsville, west of Cairns on the northeast coast of Australia). He's got the wings off, but you can put those back in an hour. He's trying to get the museum set up. He's disappointed he didn't get the tourists he thought he would at Townsville. He was offered a million dollars for the airplane, (but) didn't sell it.

Q: Was the P-39 restored to your original colors?

A: Yes. It has grey (trim), my name (and) the crew-chief's name. He found through orders I had three kills. He painted three Rising Suns (the symbol or flag of World War Two Japan) on it and our squadron insignia, "The Flying Fiend."

Q: How did you feel when you saw it?

A: Really thrilled! I didn't think I'd see that again when I left! I walked from the airplane with Lieutenant Harvey who went down with me. I thought it was seven days, but they say it must have been three. A long way to the beach through the jungle. We camped two or three times, had a (hard) time getting to the shore, and dug a hole in the sand and covered up so the crocodiles wouldn't get us that night. (An) Australian rescue ship flew over the next day and saw us. We had a sign written in the sand that said, "Please drop food and water." He dropped a note that said, "What do you think this is, a flying restaurant?" If I had had a machine gun, I would have shot him down!

Q: When did you last fly a P-39?

A: (In) 1945 at Victorville, California. They were training pilots in P-39s. I was a returnee and flew one.

Q: What were your total hours flying the P-39?

A: I had over 200 hours when I went overseas. I was training (for) about 50 hours. I had 144 combat missions. I was getting 400 to 500 hours. In that early time, that was a lot of hours in a P-39! That stuff accumulated slowly.

Q: Any last comments?

A: I was fond of the P-39. I had a good war record, and it was the P-39 I got the war record in. I watched a lot of people crash the P-39. I know why they crashed: they couldn't handle it. Some were scared of it, some weren't good pilots, and some were considered too inexperienced to fly any fighter under the conditions. (For) those that had stateside training, it was a normal transfer of airplanes. It had nothing to do with the war. (We) started training in it. I couldn't ask for better. Of course, when I got the P-38 and I'd get to altitude, I could see the difference in performance. The P-38 had a supercharger and it would go up there. You could get things done. I don't know anything about the P-39 in the other theatres because I wasn't there. Against the Japanese, it wasn't the greatest weapon because of the altitude you had to fly to get their bombers which were doing most of the damage. It (the P-39) just wouldn't go up and do it. But it was a great airplane, and its presence in New Guinea deterred the Japanese from landing in Australia, I can guarantee that. The P-39 did that; it wasn't other airplanes. I have nothing but praise for the P-39, but you had to know what you were doing to handle it, or you would kill yourself.

Thank you, Colonel Falletta.

Brigadier General Chuck Yeager

World War Two Fighter Pilot and Ace

General Yeager is world-famous not only as a World War Two fighter pilot and ace, but as the first person to break the sound barrier. The first fighter plane he flew, however, was the Bell P-39 Airacobra. Our last interview is with General Yeager about his Airacobra experiences.

Q: General Yeager, when did you first fly the P-39?

A: Around March 20, 1943.

Q: Was this in training at Tonopah, Nevada (in south central Nevada, midway between Reno and Las Vegas)?

A: Yes.

*Q: I reviewed your autobiography (*Yeager, An Autobiography, *by General Chuck Yeager and Leo Janos, Bantam Books/July 1985) earlier. When did you train in the P-39?*

A: We started at Tonopah in the 363rd Fighter Squadron around the 20th of March, and we flew the airplane until the middle of November 1943. I got about 500 total hours in the airplane.

Q: You mentioned your first introduction to flying the P-39 was a brief instruction by Bill O'Brien?

A: Yes. That's the way all single-seat fighters were in those days. Instructors would talk to you while you sat in the cockpit and went through the systems. Then you flew it.

Q: Did you fly a TP-39, the two-seat trainer conversion P-39?

A: I never knew they existed. In fact, I still don't!

Q: In this book's earlier interviews, there were references to P-39 stall problems. Do you feel the same way?

A: No. The airplane was honest stalling. There is no documented evidence the airplane would tumble. I've talked to many Bell test pilots such as Dick Frost who is mentioned in my autobiography. He was one of the test pilots on the P-39. He states Bell could never document a tumble with the P-39. It was an honest airplane in stalling whether it was a high-speed stall or a straight-away stall. You can stall any airplane, or add 5 or 10 miles per hour to that stall speed to figure out your landing speed and be in good shape.

Q: What was good about the P-39?

A: The P-39 had tricycle gear, so it was very easy to handle on landing. Second, the visibility from the airplane was outstanding. Third, it carried tremendous armament. Finally, it was a very agile airplane for air-to-ground work or dogfighting as long as you stayed below 10,000 feet.

Q: Were there any negative characteristics?

A: No. I have no negative feelings about the P-39. I would have gladly gone into combat in it. Whether or not I would have been any good in combat with it is speculation. But unfortunately the airplane, not being equipped with a two-stage blower, wasn't good at altitude.

Q: Some interviews said the guns, especially the 37mm cannon, were very reliable, while others said the cannon would jam after one, two or three shots being fired?

A: You could charge the guns, both the 37mm or the 20mm if you had a 20, or the .50s (calibre machine guns) manually if they jammed. We never had problems.

General Yeager, April 1990, at McDonnell Douglas Corp. in St. Louis, Missouri, with F-15E Number 1. COURTESY GENERAL YEAGER AND McDONNELL DOUGLAS CORPORATION.

I was the maintenance officer in my squadron and worked on the airplanes. I was aware of the complaints the guys had about the airplane. It was a good airplane. Most rumors about the P-39 are from pilots who never flew the airplane! It's hearsay.

Q: Did you fire the 37mm cannon frequently?

A: Yes. We fired air-to-ground a lot while at Tonopah and later at every place we were stationed with the airplane, and especially at Casper, Wyoming (in east central Wyoming, near the Laramie Mountains) where we flew them for the last time. We had air-to-ground ranges where we had life-size silhouette targets of tanks, trucks and airplanes on the ground. You could fly the course with 15 or 20 different targets laid out. It would take a few minutes to get through. We fired the 37mm a lot. I loved the gun. Because the 37mm did not have a high velocity cartridge, we had a lot of trajectory involved with it, but it was a good gun.

Q: Do you know why there were complaints of frequent jams in combat from people who flew the P-39, some with many missions?

A: I don't know. I never had that problem. Most who had the jamming I'm sure either had poor maintenance or didn't know how to operate the 37mm cannon.

Q: What P-39 models did you fly?

A: We flew the N and the L. I'd have to go to my Form 5. That's the only place they listed the models. I flew P-39s through the Q which had the Aeroproducts prop. There was also a D model. Those are the ones that stick in my mind: the D, the L and the Q. Maybe there was an N or two.

Q: Did you fly any photo-reconnaissance versions?

A: No. I was unaware they existed. I did fly the P-63 when I returned from the war, but not before I went overseas. I also flew the "pinball machine" (modified P-63 Kingcobras used for practice gunnery when flown against American bomber crews) two or three times, but they were very heavy (due to heavy additional metal skinning), and I wasn't impressed!

Q: After Tonopah, you were assigned to Wright Field for service testing a new proposed propeller for the P-39?

A: Yes. That was a hollow stainless steel prop. It didn't add a lot to the airplane. It was something new.

Q: How many flight test hours did you have at Wright Field?

A: About 150. I was there a month and a half.

Q: Would you expand upon when you bailed out of a P-39 in Casper, Wyoming?

A: I was (at) 400 miles per hour and running high power. The impeller let go in the engine. There was an explosion that blew fire and debris from under the seat. It happened so fast I merely jettisoned the door and rolled out of the airplane.

Q: How well did the door release mechanism work?

A: Fine. No problem.

Q: Was your group commander in a mid-air collision losing the tail section of his P-39?

A: Yes. He went into a flat spin. As I recall his story, he jumped out the door and hit flat on the wing. He stood up and jumped off the wing!

Q: Was Casper, Wyoming, your last P-39 assignment?

A: Yes, as a unit, but I flew them later. The first one I flew after I came back from the war in Europe was Betty Haas' P-39. I took a (Republic) P-84 (Thunderjet, a sub-sonic early military single-seat jet fighter with a straight wing and one jet engine) to Philadelphia in 1946 for an air show. Since I liked the airplane, Betty Haas mentioned that that was her P-39. I said to her, "Would you mind if I sat in the cockpit? I really love the airplane!" She said, "That's unusual because most pilots didn't like the P-39." I said to her, "I never heard that! Most guys in my squadron enjoyed them." She let me fly it in an air show there.

Q: I interviewed her. You must have flown a very impressive sequence that day!

A: They thought she was flying! We got a wig and cap. I flew the show. She got in the airplane and taxied from the other runway where we changed places. Most WASPs weren't trained in aerobatics. I put on a show with the airplane: I rolled it on takeoff, did loops and cuban eights. She didn't know a P-39 could do that! I hadn't flown one for three or four years.

Q: She said you landed far enough away to give you two an opportunity to switch the parachute?

A: Yes. That's right!

Q: Did the people who picked her up in the car learn about your flying the routine?

A: No. They were surprised she could do acrobatics in the airplane, and of course, we just kept that a secret!

Q: Have you seen her since?

A: Yes. I saw her at air shows with her P-39 because, like I mentioned in my book, in those days of '46 and '47, Bob Hoover and I put on air shows practically every weekend with either (Lockheed) P-80s (the Shooting Star, another sub-sonic early jet fighter) or P-51s, or anything we could have fun with.

Q: Were those air shows for the benefit of a company or the United States government?

A: They were sponsored by the Civil Air Patrol. They were military air shows. I'm a military guy. I've never flown for any company except after I retired from the Air Force when I started doing work with the

(Northrop) F-20 (Tigershark, one of the most advanced jet fighter plane designs today).

Q: You discuss in your book visiting Russia in 1959 with Jacqueline Cochran (a famous lady aviator who set a world speed record of 652 miles per hour in May 1953 in an F-86 Sabre Jet, one of America's most famous swept-winged jet fighter planes), having dinner with Russian pilots and telling stories about flying the P-39. If I may quote your book for a moment: "They were delighted that I had flown hundreds of hours in an airplane they loved. They sure as hell didn't think we had sent them a dog."

A: That's something I've never understood. Where do such negative reports come from? Those who say "the airplane would tumble" normally have never flown or tried to tumble it. Second, I think the bad word comes from people who have never flown or gotten intimately familiar with the P-39.

Q: Yes. Did you discuss the P-39 with former Russian pilots?

A: There were a few who had flown the P-39s. They were interested in our (Lockheed) F-104s (Starfighters, capable of nearly twice the speed of sound) trying to obtain information about what we had been doing with (jet engine) compressor stalls. You can't discuss those things, so the discussion shredded out into P-39s and fun flying instead of trying to get secrets.

Q: Were they giving good feedback on the P-39?

A: Yes, from those who had flown it. They enjoyed it. It was a good tank-buster. But if you talk to guys like Erich Hartmann (a leading German Luftwaffe ace from World War Two with numerous victories in Bf-109s) or guys that flew the '109 on the Eastern Front against the Soviets, they ate the P-39 up! They shot down hundreds of them which is to be expected against an agile airplane like the '109.

Q: In your discussion with Betty Haas, there is a quote in your book where you told her the P-39 "was the best airplane I ever flew."

A: Yes. It was the first fighter I flew, but it wasn't as good as the P-51. I don't think I met Betty Haas until I returned from the war, so that wouldn't have been a valid statement because the P-39 wasn't as good as the P-51.

Q: Did the P-39 meet the need it was designed for during the first year or two of the war?

A: It was surpassed by technology, but when that's the only airplane you've got to fly, you do the best you can with it. That happens in any war. It's like the Germans shooting down early French or Italian fighters, or the P-39 being caught by the Japanese in the South Pacific. It is also like the P-38. The '38 was, unfortunately, a dismal failure in Europe. German fighter pilots shot down more P-38s that any other American fighter. But when the American forces took P-38s to the South Pacific, they did well because they were flying against a different foe. That's what happened with the P-39. It's according to who you put it against.

Q: Did you fly the Confederate Air Force's P-39 a year or two ago?

A: Yes.

Q: How was it to fly a P-39 again?

A: The '39 is a very easy airplane to fly because of the tricycle gear. It's not the most powerful airplane in the world because of its lesser horsepower. It was fun to get in the airplane and detect its characteristics I learned with the P-39s in '43. When I flew the Confederate Air Force's plane at Las Vegas, Nevada, that was the first time I had been in a P-39 since 1946 or 1947. That's a long time!

Q: Was it like putting your foot in an old shoe?

A: Yes, but I have flown so many different airplanes that I have developed my own technique. I can sit in the cockpit and think through the systems, and then fall right into it.

Q: How long did you fly the Confederate Air Force's P-39?

A: For about 45 minutes.

Q: If the opportunity came again, would they let you fly it?

A: Yes, I think they would. It's like you say, the only flying P-39 in the world and it's a valuable airplane! I was happy they had enough confidence in my ability to let me fly it. It is a single cockpit airplane, but on the other hand, I brought the F-20 and I had been flying a P-51 in the show, so they said, "Here, go fly the '39!"

Q: Did you fly acrobatics?

A: Yes. I did a few rolls, but I basically was fooling around with the airplane! When I landed, I probably touched down at ten miles per hour above the stall speed, but I could have landed slower!

Q: About a year or two ago, the aviation magazines noted the possibility of making a movie about your early years flying combat in P-51s. Is that project still alive?

A: Yes. There is some action among two or three producers. They are negotiating with my agent about buying the movie rights to my autobiography. What has also developed is that you can build quarter scale models of any airplane that's flown and make it look very realistic, and because there are so few P-39s, if you wanted to cover that period, we can go to quarter-scale models. If the movie calls for shooting down '109s or (Focke Wulf) 190s (another later Luftwaffe piston-engine fighter plane) in a war scene, you can make quarter scale models that look very realistic.

Q: If that project is done, will they cover your P-39 years?

A: I'm sure they would, yes.

Q: Would the Confederate Air Force's or the Kalamazoo Air Museum's P-39 be involved in the project?

A: It's a matter of how much money they want whereas the film company can build scale models and do as good a job with them, and probably cheaper without the risk factor. Did you say there is a P-39 in Kalamazoo?

Q: Yes. There was a second P-39 in the Confederate Air Force painted as a P-400. It was bought by the Kalamazoo Air Museum. There are others that will be flying, not maybe soon, but they are working towards that.

A: Yes. But, what happens is they rebuild these airplanes. Then the guys that fly them just don't know what they're doing, and they cream them. That's been the case with a lot of restored airplanes. It's unfortunate, but that's the way it works.

General Yeager, thank you for your interview.

A training P-39N-5 at Tonopah, Nevada, similar to the kind described in General Yeager's interview. Note the underwing bomb rails beneath the fuselage. BELL AIRCRAFT CORP. VIA TRUMAN A. PARTRIDGE, SR.

Another view of four the 312th Fighter Squadron's Airacobras. BELL AIRCRAFT CORP. VIA TRUMAN A. PARTRIDGE, SR.

AIRACOBRA SURVIVORS

Another goal established for this history was to locate as many surviving Airacobra examples as possible. Now that we have outlined the P-39's history and presented the personal accounts of those actively involved with the Airacobra, the next question the reader may ask is, "Where can I see one?"

This section presents the results an extensive search to locate the world's remaining P-39s and P-400s. The following Airacobras are by no means the absolute last few that exist. The author knows there are others sitting derelict in the underbrush of Papua New Guinea slowly returning to the elements or under the icy waters of Alaska, and elsewhere, all waiting to be rescued before totally disintegrating. What we present here are the known and reasonably confirmed survivors that have been located and are now restored or in the process of being restored.

By the late 1960s, several aircraft collectors and museums had identified two air fields in northern Papua New Guinea where many Airacobras and other American warplanes had been abandoned by the United States Army Air Force near the end of World War Two. These were Tsili Tsili and Tadji, located in West Sepik in northern Papua New Guinea, not far from the port of Aitape on the Bismark Bay. Several P-39s were recovered by collectors and museums in Australia and Papua New Guinea which were restored for display.

Nearly half of the following surviving P-39s owe their existence to David Tallichet who owns Specialty Restaurants, Inc. in Anaheim, California. He is an avid warbird collector who was a World War Two B-17 bomber pilot with 21 missions to his credit. In the late '60s or early '70s, Mr. Tallichet established an organization called Yesterday's Air Force. At one time, YAF had branches in Kansas and Florida, but by 1987, these had broken off. The group in Kansas became the Combat Air Force, but the group in Florida retained the name of Yesterday's Air Force. Mr. Tallichet renamed his group the Military Aircraft Restoration Corporation, or MARC. MARC is Tallichet's workshop and storage location based at world famous Chino Airport in California, which is probably the United States' most concentrated center for warbird restoration. MARC is part of David Tallichet's business conglomerate. MARC has today probably over 150 World War Two vintage bombers and fighters at Chino, many of which were recovered from various Pacific Islands. Some have been restored by MARC whereas others were sold to collectors with a few warbirds being donated. Aircraft stored at MARC include P-38s, P-39s, P-40s, P-47s, Spitfires, Corsairs, Avengers, Sea Furys, Skyraiders, A-26s, B-17s, B-25s, B-26s, DC-3s and T-28s. MARC restores some planes for display at Mr. Tallichet's Specialty Restaurants. Others are leased to television or movie companies for scenes requiring World War Two bombers or fighters. During 1990, the major motion picture *Memphis Belle* was released. The B-17 playing the title role was 44-83546, civilian registration N3703G, a B-17G-85DL which was modified to B-17F configuration for the filming during summer 1989 in England. N3703G belongs to David Tallichet who flew it to England for the filming.

In 1972 or 1973, David Tallichet financed a World War Two aircraft recovery expedition to Tsili Tsili and Tadji in Papua New Guinea to locate vintage warbirds. Working with d'E.C. Darby and N. M. (Monty) Armstrong of Melbourne, Australia, Tallichet's team spent six weeks locating, disassembling and removing nearly fifty different abandoned aircraft. These planes were stricken from our Army Air Force's records during 1944 and 1945 and abandoned. At least thirteen mostly P-39Ns and some P-39Qs were in the reclaimed survivors. They were sitting on air fields overgrown with underbrush. The recovered Airacobras had few visible markings and serial numbers after years of neglect, along with torn fabric on their control surfaces, smashed glass and many pieces stripped off, all because of weather and vandalism. To complicate matters, the recovered fuselages and wings were mixed during disassembly and shipment from Aitape to California, and mixed again upon storage at Chino Airport. As the reader can imagine, this mixing of parts among the recovered Airacobras has caused more than a little confusion among the museums and collectors who have these recovered ex-Tallichet P-39s. In the years that followed, many of the Tallichet P-39s were restored, sold or donated. A few still remain at MARC. In addition to David Tallichet's P-39s, N. M. Armstrong kept two Airacobras in Australia. Their stories are included in this survivors section as best they could be researched.

Our list begins with the oldest known surviving Airacobra by serial number and works to the newest. What is presented is what is known about each airplane and reasonably verified. The author welcomes any updates, changes or additional data available on these or additional Airacobras. Remember that of the 9,558

Airacobras built through 1944, only 35 survive throughout the world. That is a mere three and a half tenths of one percent of the total! For some variants such as the P-39C, P-39J and P-39L, there are *no* surviving examples. No one knows what happened to the XP-39 nor any of the YP-39s. Today, there are only two of the 35 Airacobras flying. Let's hope that more of those other 33 take to the skies once again.

The U.S. Military Aircraft Museum's P-400

The United States Military Aircraft Museum (2601 Bow Street, Jackson, Michigan 49203) is restoring an export P-400 Airacobra, (British) serial number AP 335. This is the oldest known Airacobra. Several requests for direct information about this Airacobra were not successful. Other sources state this P-400 is a former 36th Fighter Squadron, 8th Fighter Group Airacobra. It made a wheels up landing on August 2, 1943 after its coolant system was hit near Tsili Tsili by Japanese fighter interceptors. AP 335 was recovered at Bulldog, an abandoned emergency landing area located on the Lakekamu River in the Gulf Province. Its last pilot is not known. AP 335 was severely vandalized over the years. This museum bought AP 335 in 1968, but several trips to Papua New Guinea were needed before bringing the Airacobra to the United States. Colonel Jack Taft (Retired) of the museum cleared the growth around AP 335. On November 30, 1984, a Royal Australian Air Force Boeing CH-47 Chinook helicopter recovered the Airacobra and took it to Jackson's Airport at Port Moresby, 125 miles away. This P-400's export was allowed as Colonel Taft had donated funds for the restoration of another P-400, AP 347, which remained in Papua New Guinea. AP 335 came to Michigan in 1985. It is now under restoration, but to what extent or whether AP 335 will fly again is not known. This museum has approximately six aircraft. It is only accessible by prior permission. No photographs were made available.

The National Museum of Papua New Guinea's P-400

The National Museum of Papua New Guinea (Independence Drive, Waigani, Papua New Guinea) has two Airacobras in its collection according to other, unconfirmed sources. This one is a P-400 with serial number AP 347. As other unconfirmed information is reported, when the United States Military Aircraft Museum negotiated to recover and bring AP 335 to America, they also agreed to recover AP 347 and turn

All Bell Model 14 Airacobra Is had British three-color camouflage as seen on this test model in Buffalo. When later returned to the Army Air Corps, American insignia was added, and the plane was referred to as a P-400. The British serial numbers and camouflage were retained. BELL AIRCRAFT CORP. VIA TRUMAN A. PARTRIDGE, SR.

it over to the National Museum of PNG. AP 347 is another 36th Fighter Squadron, 8th Fighter Group P-400. It made a successful wheels-down landing at Bulldog on August 20, 1943, when its engine lost power due to two failed cylinders on the left side. It was then apparently abandoned. Its last pilot is not known. AP 347 was also severely vandalized. It was successfully recovered by an RAAF Chinook on November 29, 1984, and taken to Jackson's Airport after Colonel Taft earlier cleared the growth near it. AP 347 was taken to the National Museum in 1985. Despite several letters to the museum, no replies were ever received, nor were any photographs made available. The aircraft's existence and its status cannot be confirmed. One unconfirmed source states this P-400 is in a derelict condition.

Guadalcanal's P-400

Extremely sketchy and unconfirmed information states that a P-400, serial number BW 157, is in a museum located at an unspecified address on Guadalcanal. It reportedly belonged to the 67th Pursuit Squadron and was recovered by 1974. The plane's exact condition is not known despite attempts made to locate this export Airacobra. No photographs are available.

Solomon Islands' Two P-400s

Additional sketchy and unconfirmed information states a derelict P-400 is at Betikana High School War Museum with another P-400 at the Vilu Cultural Village and Museum. Both are near Honiara. Their military serial numbers are not known.

N. M. Armstrong's P-39D

As stated in the introduction, Mr. N. M. Armstrong of Victoria, Australia, assisted in recovering numerous P-39s from Papua New Guinea, many of which went to David Tallichet's Yesterday's Air Force in 1972 or 1973. Mr. Armstrong reportedly kept two Airacobras. This particular Airacobra is a P-39D, Army Air Force serial number 41-6802, Bell construction number 141. 41-6802 was delivered on August 29, 1941, under aircraft order W-535-AC-15675 at a cost of $47,842. It was first taken to Patterson Field in Ohio, but transferred to Mitchel Field, New York, by October 9, 1941. On December 15, 1941, it was transferred to Hillsgrove, and then by January 4, 1942, to Providence, Rhode Island, most likely for anti-submarine or coastal patrol. By early February 1942, 41-6802 was sent to San Francisco for shipment overseas, departing in early March 1942 mostly likely for Australia. It was stricken from the active inventory by October 31, 1944. Attempts were unsuccessful to confirm other data. Other sources state this P-39 was recovered in 1972 or 1973 and presumably restored to static condition, but how extensively is not known. In 1979, 41-6802 may have been loaned to the Museum of Transport and Technology in Auckland, New Zealand, east of Australia. In 1988, this P-39D was reportedly returned to Mr. Armstrong, but its present location is not confirmed. No photographs were made available.

Syd Beck's P-39D

Syd Beck and his Cairns (on the northeastern Australian coast) Aircraft Recovery Team, based at Mareeba (west of Cairns), Australia (C-1 P. O. Mareeba, Queensland 4880, Australia) are the proud owners of a statically restored P-39D, Army Air Force serial number 41-6951. This is the Airacobra that crash landed in Australia as described in the interview with Colonel Charles Falletta. 41-6951 began its life as Bell construction number 290 with aircraft order W-535-AC-13675 at a cost of $47,852. It was delivered on October 21, 1941. It arrived at Chanute Field, Illinois, on December 5, 1941. On January 16, 1942, 41-6951 went to Patterson Field, Ohio. It was next taken to San Francisco, California in early February 1942 and sent overseas. It was shipped to Australia on board the freighter *Maru*, and arrived in March 1942. This P-39D was assembled in Australia at Lowood. Soon after, 41-6951 was assigned to Lieutenant Charles Falletta who painted his wife's name, Erminie, on the left door. In April 1942, Falletta and five other experienced pilots flew their P-39s to Port Moresby, Papua New Guinea for combat observation with a P-40 squadron from the Royal Australian Air Force. 41-6951 is believed to be the first American combat aircraft to land in Papua New Guinea at Port Moresby during the war. After this brief tour, Falletta's group returned to Townsville, Australia to train their less experienced pilots. Two weeks later on May 1, 1942, Lieutenant Falletta and his P-39D, 41-6951, along with five P-39Fs, among them 41-7215 flown by Lieutenant Walter Harvey, were ordered to Port Moresby as replacements. The flight of six headed north, flying the Australian coast. As they did, however, the weather worsened with heavy clouds and lowering visibility. The flight last refueled at Horn Island. All six were equipped with droptanks. They flew into the diminishing weather but eventually turned back to northeastern Australia. When they could not reach Cooktown on the northeast coast, they jettisoned their belly tanks. Lieutenant

A highly censored Airacobra photo, probably of a P-39D. The tail number has been blocked out and the Army Air Corps markings have been touched up. Probably used as a publicity picture. BELL AIRCRAFT CORP. VIA TRUMAN A. PARTRIDGE, SR.

Falletta instructed the group to make forced landings at Bamaga, a sparsely populated area with clearings free of grassy scrub growth. Falletta landed wheels down first with 41-6951 about eight miles inland on the Cape York Peninsula. When his P-39D was almost stopped, the uneven ground tore his P-39D's left main landing gear out. Falletta radioed to Lieutenant Walter Harvey, his wingman in P-39F 41-7215, to make a wheels up landing, which Harvey did. Lieutenant Falletta ordered the other four pilots to land on the beach. Three made wheels up landings and lived, but the last pilot tried a wheels down landing. This was a Lieutenant Love who unfortunately was killed when his P-39F flipped over on the sand. Falletta and Harvey walked from the scrubland and were rescued by a launch on the beach. 41-6951 was finally stricken from the Army Air Force's inventory on October 31, 1944. Both pilots are alive today.

Thirty years passed with 41-6951 and 41-7215 relatively untouched in the grassy scrublands of northeastern Australia. At one point, however, a brush fire occurred, and the paint and fabric on the control surfaces of 41-6951 were burned.

In September 1972, the Cairns Aircraft Recovery Group, a team of volunteers led by Syd Beck, reclaimed both aging Airacobras. They had live 37mm shells in their cannons which could not be safely removed, and a demolition team from the Royal Australian Air Force was called. Using plastic explosives, the upper forward fuselages of both P-39s were blown apart, severely damaging the cockpits. Both were then trucked from the scrublands on flatbeds to the east coast, placed on a ship to Cairns, and trucked again the final 240 miles to the Townsville Aero Museum. 41-6951 remained there until 1987 while being restored. Its wings had little damage, but the spars were corroded and needed changing. Repair assistance came from the Australian Aircraft Restoration Group in Melbourne at the Moorabbin Aviation Museum. By July 1980, the engine bay was restored. A new Allison V-1710-35 engine was installed and test run later that month. By January 1982, the damaged nose section remained. Syd Beck and his volunteers spent twelve days searching the Australian coastline by trawler. They located seven crashed or waterlanded Airacobras near Queensland. The team removed usable nose pieces from the wrecks. The parts were badly corroded but served as templates for new parts that were handmade for 41-6951. The nose section was essentially remanufactured by August 1982. The repaired propeller was added in January 1983 with Colonel Falletta assisting during a visit. By 1984, this P-39D had all cockpit instrumentation. By 1987, 41-6951 was completed and moved to a hangar at the Mareeba Aero Museum where it is on static display to the public. Photographs of 41-6951 were requested, but none were made available.

The National Museum of Papua New Guinea's P-39D

Along with P-400 serial number AP 347, the National Museum of Papua New Guinea is believed to have a P-39D, Army Air Force serial number 41-6970, Bell construction number 309. 41-6970 was delivered on October 30, 1941 under aircraft order W-535-AC-15675 at a cost of $47,852. It was transferred to Chanute Field, Illinois, on November 19, 1941, and then to Patterson Field, Ohio, on January 16, 1942. It arrived in San Francisco, California, in early February 1942 and was shipped overseas in March 1942. It was stricken from the Army Air Force inventory on October 31, 1944. Several requests for information and photographs were unsuccessful. 41-6970 was reportedly recovered in the late 1960s or early 1970s in Papua New Guinea. The extent of restoration is not known although it is presumably in a static condition. It reportedly went on display in 1982, but another unconfirmed source states the Airacobra is in a derelict condition.

The Soviet Union's P-39D or P-39Q

Despite several thousand P-39s sent to Russia under Lend-Lease during World War Two and checking numerous sources, one unconfirmed source states a P-39D is in the Central Museum of the Armed Forces in Moscow as of 1986, whereas another says there is an unidentified P-39Q at the Pouryshkin Museum in Novosibirsk on display as of 1988 or 1989. Neither the Army Air Force nor Russian serial numbers are known. These Airacobras are believed to exist, but are not confirmed. No photographs are available.

Nick Watling's P-39F, 41-7215, as seen when recovered after the ammunition in the forward fuselage had been destroyed.
COURTESY NICK WATLING

Nick Watling's P-39F

Nick Watling of Smithfield Heights, Queensland, Australia, owns the P-39F, Army Air Force serial number 41-7215, flown by Lieutenant Walter Harvey that crash landed after Lieutenant Falletta at Bamaga, Australia. 41-7215 was delivered on January 23, 1942 with Bell construction number 15-554. It cost $47,842 under aircraft order W535-AC-15675. It was shipped by crate to Australia with the *Pensacola* convoy. It was assembled at Eagle Farm in Brisbane, Australia, in March or April 1942. It served with an operational training unit at Lowood, north of Brisbane. From there it went to Antil Plains, ten miles south of Townsville.

Photos of Watling's P-39F taken in 1988 before 41-7215 was placed in temporary storage. An absolutely first-class restoration in progress. COURTESY NICK WATLING

Lieutenant Harvey was Falletta's wingman during that fateful flight on May 1, 1942. 41-7215 made a wheels up landing at Falletta's direction, bending the propeller in the process. It was stricken from the inventory on October 31, 1944. 41-7215 was abandoned and forgotten for thirty years. It was removed from the scrublands by the Cairns Aircraft Recovery Team in November 1971. Nick Watling then became its owner. Much of the restoration of 41-7215 has been done by Ian Mullins who knew about this crashed Airacobra as far back as 1960. Restoration began on 41-7215 in August 1972 in Cairns and progressed until May 1975 when the Airacobra was taken to Mount Isa in western Queensland, Australia for continuing repairs until 1988. Work was temporarily stopped in 1988, and 41-7215 was placed in storage at Mossman until Ian Mullins retired in Townsville in 1990. Mossman is 40 miles north of Cairns and Mareeba where 41-6951 is located.

By 1988, half of all restoration work on 41-7215 was completed. The fuselage, cockpit, rear section and tail plane were restored, and the Allison engine had been overhauled. The wings, however, remained in the same stored condition as they were when recovered in 1971. 41-7215 will use a fiberglas propeller as there are no replacements in Australia. The cockpit is finished and beautifully detailed. This Airacobra will hopefully be completed to a static display condition (due to difficulties replacing the center section and wing spars) by 1995. It will probably be returned to its original paint scheme. Mr. Watling plans to place 41-7215 on display at the Cairns airport.

Bob Jarrett's P-39K-1

Bob Jarrett of Salisbury East, South Australia is the owner of the only surviving P-39K in the world, Army Air Force serial number 42-4312. This P-39K was delivered on July 31, 1942, with twelve flying hours under aircraft order W535-AC-20910 at a cost of $48,673. It was transferred by land to San Francisco for overseas shipment in August, arriving most likely in Australia. It was later based on Fiji Island. This P-39K is believed to have been with the 39th Fighter Squadron flying from Narewa air field on Woodlark Island, Papua New Guinea, which is in the Solomon Sea east of Port Moresby, southeast of Papua New Guinea. On March 18, 1943, 42-4312 was wrecked at Narewa. The pilot was Sergeant Frank H. Cranston who was killed while completing a ground crew check. Although the Army Air Force accident report is not available, according to Mr. Jarrett, a "careful examination of the fuselage damage explains the probable sequence of events. The aircraft was not airborne as there is no underside damage. The noseleg undercarriage was known to be laterally unstable. The retract gear displayed shows the broken retract arm. This occurred when the undercarriage leg collapsed sideways. This resulted in the turning propeller hitting the ground which broke the driveshaft loose at the center bearing assembly in the cockpit. Severe impact damage by the driveshaft on the cockpit floor and shaft-carrying casting and the exclusion of any other cockpit damage indicate that Sergeant Cranston may have succumbed to injuries as a result of a collapsed nosewheel oleo leg while taxiing the aircraft." This P-39K then became a parts plane. It was condemned on November 3, 1943, and stricken from the inventory on April 1, 1944. It was abandoned on Woodlark Island.

Bob Jarrett learned of 42-4312 after it was found in the jungle growth at Narewa Field on Woodlark Island. He purchased it in 1982 when it was in a corroded condition. It had no motor, doors, engine covers or glass. Bob Jarrett has completed 70 percent of the rebuilding on this last P-39K to restore it for static display. He said it is "an enormous job, but most satisfying." Most exterior reskinning is completed on the fuselage and tail section. The original wing was too corroded for rebuilding, so the wing from a P-39D, Army Air Force serial number 42-4368, will be rebuilt for 42-4312. This P-39K has been displayed during restoration for several years at the South Australian Aviation Museum. Its fuselage is missing the doors and plexiglas. The wing has been removed and is partially completed. The fuselage needs a propeller and reduction gearbox. This Airacobra will be repainted as a 39th Fighter Squadron P-39K. Its estimated completion date is 1994.

Photos of the last P-39K-1 left in the world, taken from the time it was pulled out of the jungle to the present. An incredible undertaking. COURTESY BOB JARRETT

Don Whittington's P-39

Don Whittington of World Jet Company (Fort Lauderdale, Florida) has a P-39 of an unknown description. Despite several attempts, few details of its restoration were obtained, not even the serial number. It was described as a "complete airplane" that has "never been apart." Reportedly this Airacobra was forgotten in a park. It was periodically given a coat of paint before Mr. Whittington recovered it. No photographs were made available.

MARC's P-39N-0

Military Aircraft Restoration Corporation (7000 Merrill Avenue, Box 37, Chino, California 91710) has several P-39s recovered from Papua New Guinea, but one P-39N, Army Air Force serial number 42-4949, had a different recovery location. This Airacobra was reportedly recovered in November 1971 from Fort Nelson, British Columbia, Canada. 42-4949 was delivered on December 7, 1942, under aircraft order W535-AC-20910 at a cost of $48,673. On December 9, 1942, it was taken to Bell's Modification Center. Records show it was sent to Alaska, so the Modification Center must have added additional equipment for cold-weather usage. On February 4, 1943, 42-4949 arrived at Great Falls, Montana. It next went to Ladd Field on February 13, 1943. It was transferred to Elmendorf Field, Alaska by May 11, 1943. It was stricken from the inventory by May 6, 1944. It most likely crashed in Canada between May 1943 and May 1944. Very little information exists on it. It was based at MARC from its recovery in 1971 to at least 1979. It supposedly still exists there. As with all P-39s at MARC, several attempts were made to confirm these MARC/Tallichet Airacobras, but no confirming responses were supplied. No photographs were made available.

The Yankee Air Corps' P-39N-O-BE

The Yankee Air Corps (7000 Merrill Avenue, Box 35, Chino, California 91710) maintains an excellent reputation for aircraft restoration. They are restoring a P-39N-O-BE, Army Air Force serial number 42-8740 (reported erroneously elsewhere as 42-8881, a P-39N-O delivered on December 26, 1942, that flew with the 328th Fighter Group and crashed on March 1, 1943 north of Hamilton Field, California, when Lieutenant Edward Tanner's engine failed, the cockpit filled with smoke, and the pilot bailed out successfully. 42-8881 was stricken from the records on March 2, 1943).

A standard P-39N-1 on the Bell ramp at Buffalo during World War Two. The "N" was Bell's first large-scale Airacobra order.
BELL AIRCRAFT CORP. VIA TRUMAN A. PARTRIDGE, SR.

42-8740, Yankee's correct P-39N-O, was delivered on December 7, 1942, under aircraft order W535-AC-20910 at a cost of $48,673. It was taken by land to depart from Brooklyn, New York, on December 21, 1942. Its service history is not known although it may have served with the British in Australia or New Guinea. 42-8740 is an ex-Tallichet P-39 recovered from Tadji airstrip by April 1972. It was in better condition when recovered than other P-39s. 42-8740 went to a restoration group in Oklahoma that completed some of the Airacobra's repairs and exterior reskinning. In March 1989, Yankee Air Corps obtained 42-8740 in a disassembled condition though a trade. By now it had civilian registration number N81575. Yankee began a complete restoration to return the P-39 to flying condition. By the end of 1989, the cockpit section was completed with excellent results. Presently 42-8740 has its wings off. All fuselage and tail section members have been reskinned. Some replacement parts have been added from other P-39s beyond repair. 42-8740 will receive an Aeroproducts propeller which Yankee has. This Airacobra will be painted in olive drab and pale grey with United States markings. It is 40 percent completed to airworthy standards. No photographs were available although Yankee is keeping a video record of their restoration.

Other MARC P-39Ns

MARC has several P-39Ns in California and New York with sketchy backgrounds which were recovered from Papua New Guinea as earlier described. These aircraft are Army Air Force serial numbers 42-18403, 42-18408, 42-18811, 42-18814, 42-19034 and a final unnumbered P-39N-5. One P-39N is believed to be Ed Maloney's Airacobra on static display at his "Planes of Fame" museum.

42-18403 is a P-39N-5 delivered on March 17, 1943, under aircraft order number

The two unrestored MARC P-39 airframes at the National Warplane Heritage in April 1990.
PHOTOS BY TRUMAN A. PARTRIDGE, SR.

W535-AC-20910 at a cost of $48,673. It was taken to the Stockton International Depot by land on April 3, 1943. It next went to Fort Mason on April 21, 1943, and was sent overseas later that month. It was stricken from the records in April 1944. 42-18408 was built March 15, 1943 with the same cost, order number and shipping information. It was stricken from the inventory on May 25, 1944. 42-18811 is also a P-39N-5 but delivered on April 9, 1943 with the same cost and order number. It went to Stockton April 29, 1943, Fort Mason on May 7, 1943, and was shipped May 17, 1943. It was stricken from the inventory on April 30, 1945. 42-18814 was delivered April 12, 1943 with the same cost and order number. The rest of its data after arriving in Stockton on April 30, 1943 is identical to the prior P-39N-5. 42-19034, also a P-39N-5, was delivered on April 29, 1943 with the same cost and order number. This P-39 was shipped through the Port of Baltimore on May 4, 1943. It went overseas on May 27, 1943. It was stricken from the records on August 10, 1944.

With the exception of Ed Maloney's P-39N, no information on the extent of restoration has been supplied to the author on these Airacobras despite several requests. Two of these unrestored airframes are in storage at the National Warplane Heritage (P. O. Box 159, Geneseo, New York 14954) (although another source says these are P-39Qs and not Ns). They are shells only with little if any visible marking according to the museum's archivist. They will eventually be returned to MARC in California.

The P-39N at Planes of Fame (7000 Merrill Avenue, Chino Airport, California 91710), whose tail number has not been confirmed to the author, is described as a P-39N-5-BE, according to Mr. Maloney. There is a friendly dispute between Planes of Fame and another P-39N restorer, Fred Johnsen, as to which P-39N each has. Both claim to have 42-19027, a P-39N nicknamed "Small Fry" during the war. The problem of mixed P-39 pieces described earlier has given both owners indications they have the true "Small Fry." MARC restored Maloney's P-39N to static display, but most identification plates were missing when Planes of Fame received and later re-restored it to some extent. Planes of Fame has had their Airacobra on display since the late 1970s. It is missing some instruments and its engine, but Planes of Fame does have an Allison for it. This P-39 may be made airworthy as Planes of Fame is considered a "flying museum." Their P-39 is painted in olive drab and light grey. It does say "Small Fry" on it.

Despite several requests to all parties, no photographs were made available on any of these P-39Ns from their owners.

Frederick A. Johnsen's P-39N, "Small Fry," April 1990.
PHOTO BY FREDERICK A. JOHNSEN

Frederick A. Johnsen's P-39N

Since 1987 Fred Johnsen, the owner of Museum Aeronautica and an aviation writer in Tacoma, Washington, has owned one of the ex-Tallichet P-39Ns recovered from Papua New Guinea. His Airacobra is Army Air Force serial number 42-19027, nicknamed "Small Fry." Some parts of this Airacobra may have been mixed with other MARC recovered P-39s. "Small Fry" had one or two enemy victories to its credit as evidenced by the "kill" symbols detected on its right fuselage side. These may have been two Japanese Oscars (fighters) shot down in November 1943. 42-19027 was delivered on April 28, 1943, under Army Air Force order AC-20910 at a cost of $48,673. It was shipped by land to the Port of Baltimore on May 4, 1943. It went to Port Stockton on May 19, 1943, and Fort Mason on May 20, 1943. It was shipped overseas in late May 1943. It was in service from June 1943 until July 16, 1944, when it was stricken from the records. It served with the 35th Fighter Squadron and the 71st Tactical Reconnaissance Group. It was later abandoned at Tadji air field. This P-39N is being restored to its wartime condition. Some sheet metal restoration is being completed by the Clover Park Vocational Technical Institute in Tacoma since 1989. It is hoped this Airacobra will be returned to airworthy standards although wing spar corrosion appears a major concern.

The J. K. McCarthy Museum's P-39N-5

Located in central Papua New Guinea in the eastern highlands is the J. K. McCarthy Museum. (P. O. Box 132, Goroka, E.H.P., Papua New Guinea). This museum displays a P-39N-5, Army Air Force serial number 42-19039. According to Ivan G. M'bagintao, the museum's curator, their N-5 on display is in good condition, although no photographs were made available for this book. It is presumably a static aircraft.

42-19039 was built at a cost of $48,873 and delivered to the Army Air Force on April 29, 1943. It was built under Army Air Force order AC-20910. It was transferred to Baltimore by land on May 4, 1943, and sent to Port Stockton on May 19, 1943. It arrived at Fort Mason on May 20, 1943, and was sent overseas on May 27, 1943. It was shipped to the South Pacific to the Solomon Islands in June 1943. This P-39N-5 operated with the 82nd Tactical Reconnaissance Squadron at Dobodura (due east of Port Moresby in southeastern Papua New Guinea), Finschhaffen (eastern central coast of Papua New Guinea) and Saidor (on the northeastern coast of Papua New Guinea). It also flew out of Owi Island and Biak Island (both northwest of Irian Jaya, the western half of the major island mass that Papua New Guinea shares to the east). From Biak Island, 42-19039 was finally taken to Tadji air field in Papua New Guinea, where it served with the 110th Tactical Reconnaissance Squadron. 42-19039 was stricken from the Army Air Force's inventory on May 21, 1945, and abandoned at Tadji.

The pilot with the most combat experience in 42-19039 was Lieutenant Charles W. Borders. He flew this P-39 with the name "San Antonio Rose." His crewchief was Sergeant Eugene F. Behnkendorf. Lieutenant Borders was assigned to the 82nd Tactical Reconnaissance Squadron in November 1943 when the unit was at Dobodura. In January 1944, he flew to Torokina (on the west coast of Bougainville Island in the Solomon Islands east of Papua New Guinea), to take command of 42-19039 and return it to Dobodura. Between January and July 12, 1944, Lieutenant Borders flew 56 combat missions in "San Antonio Rose." Targets were attacked in Hollandia (northern coast of Irian Jaya), the Finisterre Mountains, along the Ramu River, western New Britain (east of Papua New Guinea) and Rabaul (the eastern coast of New Britain). Lieutenant Borders left 42-19039 at Biak Island before it was transferred to Tadji.

42-19039 was one of the earliest P-39s recovered from Tadji. In 1967, the Goroka Branch of the Air Force Association sponsored 42-19039's recovery. This P-39N-5 was dismantled and taken to Goroka by the Royal Australian Air Force. It went on display at the J. K. McCarthy Museum in the early 1970s where it remains today.

The Confederate Air Force's P-39Q-5-BE

The Confederate Air Force in Texas (headquartered at Rebel Field, P. O. Box CAF, Harlingen, Texas 78550) flies the world's premier P-39 Airacobra example, a P-39Q-5-BE, Bell construction number 21-9597, Army Air Force serial number 42-19597, also known as civilian registration number N6968. It is the *only* P-39 in the world that is flown regularly. It is impeccably maintained in flying condition and a magnificent representative Airacobra.

42-19597 was delivered to the Army Air Force on May 25, 1943, under Army Air Force order AC-20910 at a cost of $48,673. It was the second Q-5 produced. Through July 1943, 42-19597 was on loan to Bell at Buffalo. On December 29, 1943, it was flown to Cincinnati, Ohio, and transferred to Laredo, Texas, by January 1944. In April 1944, 42-19597 was converted to a two-place trainer and redesignated as a TP-39Q. By June 1944, it was transferred to Harlingen, Texas when Harlingen was an active United States Army Air Force gunnery training base, long before the Confederate Air Force, a private organization, was created. On July 2, 1945, 42-19597 was ordered on a cross country flight intended as its last trip, to a Reconstruction Finance Corporation scrapyard to be stricken off the active inventory and disposed of. Fortunately for aviation posterity, it suffered an engine failure on July 20, 1945.

These photos were taken on April 8, 1989, at the Confederate Air Force's 50th anniversary of the P-39.
COURTESY BELL HELICOPTER/TEXTRON

RIGHT: The cockpit of the CAF's P-39Q-5.

BELOW: Colonel Sansing starts the CAF's P-39 and prepares to taxi out.

Its pilot landed the crippled P-39 in Hobbs, New Mexico, at a cropdusting airstrip. The Airacobra was abandoned by the Army Air Force. The owner of the airstrip used the disabled P-39 as a parts source for maintaining his cropdusting aircraft. The Airacobra became a virtual derelict, partially dismantled and eventually forgotten about. It became a school yard display at Capitan High School in Lincoln, New Mexico. In April 1956, Colonel Chet Kochan of the Central Texas (Cen-Tex) Wing of the Confederate Air Force found the derelict behind a fence at the school. In 1962, the P-39 was donated by Joe Brown of Hobbs, New Mexico, to the CAF when the Airacobra was disassembled. Its pieces were trucked to CAF headquarters in Harlingen, Texas. At this point, the P-39 had only 392 recorded flight hours.

In 1968, Don Hull of Sugarland, Texas, began restoring 42-19597 to flying condition. All armament and armor plating were deleted. A cooling water tank and pump were added to the nose connected to a spray bar shooting water on the radiator. This is used to cool the motor until the P-39 gets airborne. A new Allison V-1710-85 engine replaced the malfunctioned unit from the end of the war. A current radio and a civilian artificial horizon were added, but no major modifications were done. Finally, 42-19597 was repainted olive drab, but with the Russian markings and the red stars trimmed in yellow of the Voenno-Vozdusney Sily, "the military aviation forces of the Soviet Union," representing so many of Bell's P-39s sent to Russia during the war under Lend-Lease. After being restored, 42-19597 was civilian registered as N6968. It flew on October 21, 1974, but the Airacobra, however, underwent a landing gear lowering failure wherein all three gears only lowered one-third. The restored P-39 suffered a belly landing but was repaired. All original factory switches and wiring were replaced with the Airacobra soon flying again.

In 1974, the founder and first leader of the Cen-Tex Wing, Colonel John Stokes, bought N6968. On December 2, 1974, he donated the restored P-39 to the Confederate Air Force. Mr. Stokes, however, has remained 42-19597's sole sponsor while the P-39 is hangared at the Central Texas (Cen-Tex) Wing of the Confederate Air Force which was formed in 1974 in San Marcos, Texas. (1825 Airport Drive, San Marcos Municipal Airport, San Marcos, Texas 78666) (40 miles northeast of San Antonio). Mr. Stokes covers all maintenance for this CAF fighter as he has done for several other CAF airplanes, along with sponsoring two full-time retired Air Force mechanics. By 1988, a fresh Allison V-1710-85 engine was added to N6968.

The most frequent pilot for N6968 for the past five years has been Virgil E. "Sandy" Sansing of New Braunfels, Texas, a retired Air Force pilot with numerous hours in propeller and jet fighter planes. His interview appeared earlier. The other CAF P-39 pilot is Colonel Bob Ayers. 42-19597 flies with a centerline belly tank that doubles the P-39's flying time. N6968 was guest flown by General Chuck Yeager in 1989 at the "Gathering of Eagles" at Las Vegas, Nevada. This Airacobra now has 800 total flying hours.

The Confederate Air Force's P-39Q-5 in its World War Two trim as seen while at Bell Aircraft Corporation in the late summer or fall of 1943.
BELL AIRCRAFT CORP. VIA TRUMAN A. PARTRIDGE, SR.

The 188th P-39Q-10 Airacobra at Bell Aircraft Corporation during the late summer of 1943.
BELL AIRCRAFT CORP. VIA TRUMAN A. PARTRIDGE, SR.

MARC's P-39Qs

In addition to P-39Ns, MARC recovered several P-39Q Airacobras. Those believed remaining at Chino Airport are 42-19991, (although one source says 41-19991 is actually one of the P-39s at the National Warplane Heritage), 42-20007, 42-20339 and 44-2438. With the exception possibly of 44-2438, all were recovered from Papua New Guinea, but no further details are known despite several attempts to locate such information. All are believed unrestored. No photographs were made available.

42-19991 was delivered on June 8, 1943, under Army Air Force order AC-20910 at a cost of $48,673. It was taken by land to the Stockton Depot on June 22, 1943, then to Fort Mason on July 10, 1943, and shipped overseas on August 16, 1943. It was stricken from the inventory on May 21, 1945. 42-20007 was delivered on June 9, 1943, for the same order and price. It was also taken by land to Stockton on July 6, 1943, Fort Mason on July 11, 1943, and shipped July 21, 1943. It was stricken from the inventory on July 16, 1944. 42-20339 was delivered on July 9, 1943, for the same order and price. It went to Stockton by land on July 15, 1943, Fort Mason on July 20, 1943, shipped August 23, 1943, and was stricken on May 21, 1945. 44-2438 was a P-39Q-15 delivered on October 30, 1943. This Airacobra may not have been sent overseas. It may have spent its military career in the Oakland, California, area. Its final disposition and when it was stricken from the inventory are not known. No other details are known about these P-39Qs.

N. M. Armstrong's P-39Q

The other Airacobra kept by N. M. Armstrong of Victoria, Australia, is a P-39Q, Army Air Force serial number 42-19993 (although one source says 42-19993 is actually one of the hulks at the National Warplane Heritage). This P-39Q was recovered from Tadji in 1972 or 1973. Photos published in the book "Pacific Wrecks" several years ago show it sitting in an overgrown field with brush growing through it. The fabric on the control surfaces, the engine, the cockpit and forward fuselage doors, and the propeller were missing. 42-19993 was delivered to the Army Air Force on June 8, 1943, at a cost of $48,673 under Army Air Force order AC-20910. It was taken by land to Stockton on June on June 27, 1943. It arrived at Fort Mason on July 6, 1943. It was shipped overseas on August 16, 1943. This P-39 served with the 82nd Tactical Reconnaissance Squadron. Its pilot was Lieutenant Peter A. McDermott, crewchief Sergeant James W. O'Mara and armorer

Sergeant John M. Conway whose painted names were visible on the decaying fuselage along with nine yellow vertical bomb symbols below the pilot's name. 42-19993 was stricken from the inventory on May 21, 1945. It was removed from Tadji in 1972 or 1973 and taken to Auckland, New Zealand, where it was stored until 1974 according to unconfirmed reports. It may have been loaned to the Museum of Transport and Technology during this time. It was apparently restored between then and 1982 when it went on static display at Essendon Airport in Melbourne, Australia. In 1989 it was moved to Drage Air World at Wangaratta, Victoria, Australia. A request for confirming information and photographs was made, but no reply was received. *(See also "Postscript" on page 118.)*

The Buffalo and Erie County Naval and Servicemen's Park's P-39Q-6

Located in the city where P-39s were built is the Buffalo and Erie County Naval and Servicemen's Park (1 Naval Park Cove, Buffalo, New York 14202). Opened in spring 1981, this museum displays suspended from its ceiling a P-39Q-6, reportedly one of 148 Q-5s modified to carry reconnaissance cameras in its lower rear fuselage, Army Air Force serial number 42-19995. This was the P-39 described earlier flown by Lieutenant Colonel Shomo in combat. 42-19995 was delivered on June 8, 1943, at a cost of $48,673 under Army Air Force order AC-20910. It was taken by land to the Stockton Depot 20, 1943, Fort Mason on June 27, 1943, and then shipped overseas on July 7, 1943 to Australia. It probably served with the 80th Fighter Squadron which turned in its P-39s before transitioning into P-38s by October 1943. 42-19995 was reassigned to the 82nd Tactical Reconnaissance Squadron of the 71st Tactical Reconnaissance Group on November 24, 1943. The

Snooks 2nd as seen in 1990 at the Buffalo and Erie County Naval and Servicemen's Park. This was Lieutenant Colonel William A. Shomo's P-39Q-6 during the war. It is now beautifully restored to static display. COURTESY NAVAL AND SERVICEMEN'S PARK

Galloping Gertie as she looked while on display at the EAA Museum. She looks the same today, but she is now at Silver Hill, Maryland, on open public display. This was Betty Haas Pfister's Airacobra in the late 1940s. COURTESY EAA MUSEUM

unit was operating from Dobodura, an air field east of Port Moresby in southeastern Papua New Guinea. The squadron was called the "Strafin' Saints," and 42-19995 was nicknamed "Betty Lou-3rd" by its former pilot. Lieutenant Shomo took command of 42-19995 by late March or early April 1944 when based at Finschaffen, on the eastern central coast of Papua New Guinea. 42-19995 was renamed *Snooks 2nd,* which was painted on the right front fuselage. *Snooks* was the family name of the wife of Shomo's crewchief, Master Sergeant Ralph E. Winkel. Shomo's first P-39, AAF serial number 42-20351, was named *Snooks*, but it was lost in another pilot's accident. Lieutenant Shomo flew *Snooks 2nd* until August 1944 when his squadron transitioned into P-40Ns. By then, Shomo and *Snooks 2nd* had flown from Saidor in northeastern Papua New Guinea as well as later from Owi Island and Biak Island, northwest of Irian Jaya to the west of Papua New Guinea. *Snooks 2nd* was later reassigned to another pilot named Charles Weber. It was struck from the Army Air Force's records and abandoned at Tadji during December 1944.

42-19995 was recovered by David Tallichet's team in 1972 or 1973. It was stored at Yesterday's Air Force until 1980. In February 1980, Buffalo attorney Anthony D. Mancinelli learned both that these P-39s had been recovered and that David Tallichet's Specialty Restaurants, Inc. was planning to build a restaurant on the Buffalo waterfront. Ten months of negotiations between these gentlemen led to this P-39Q being donated to the new museum where it arrived on December 29, 1980. The P-39 was quickly restored by a team of volunteers during the next few months. Many pieces were fabricated for the Airacobra such as doors, access panels and gun pods. One of the volunteers, Mr. Truman A. Partridge, Sr., a former illustrator with Bell Aircraft Corporation for ten years and by then an art teacher at a nearby middle school, confirmed this P-39Q was 42-19995 in March 1981. Contact was made with Lieutenant Colonel Shomo and Master Sergeant Winkel to verify the Airacobra's correct markings. This P-39Q went on restored static display on March 28, 1981. It has no engine nor instrument panel. The cockpit and fuselage are not complete. Some original sections of this P-39, such as the wing panels, may have been mixed with other Tallichet recovered P-39s, a problem faced by several ex-Tallichet P-39 owners. 42-19995 is painted olive drab and pale grey with accurate yellow trim. It was completed in time for the museum's opening. The museum is open to the public.

The National Air and Space Museum's P-39Q-15-BE

The National Air and Space Museum (located on the mall in the nation's capitol) has one Airacobra in its collection, a Bell P-39Q-15-BE, Army Air Force serial number 44-2433, Bell construction number 26E-433, currently painted in a military paint scheme with its military tail number of 42433 displayed. This Airacobra, known as *Galloping Gertie*, is not restored and is not in the downtown Washington, D.C. museum. It is at the Paul E. Garber restoration facility on open public display while in storage awaiting restoration. The Garber facility is located in Silver Hill, Maryland, southeast of the District. Tour information may be obtained by calling (202) 357-1400.

Galloping Gertie is perhaps the finest generally unrestored surviving P-39 in existence. 44-2433 was accepted by the Army Air Force on October 28, 1943. It wore a typical olive drab and neutral grey military color scheme with yellow tail numbers. It was delivered to the Army Air Corps on November 14, 1943, under contract AC-40071 at an unspecified cost. This P-39Q saw all military duty within the United States. It was assigned to a Replacement Training Unit, the 369th Fighter Group, located at Hamilton Field, California, arriving on November 21, 1943. Between August 30 and November 29, 1944, it served for brief periods at Moses Lake, Paine Field and McChord Field in Washington state. It was ferried to an unspecified Reconstruction Finance Corporation depot for disposal on December 6, 1944. When it was sold to its first civilian owner is not known. Its first owners are believed to have been the (Earl) Ortman and Mighton Aviation Company of Tulsa, Oklahoma. They paid $750 for this P-39. Ortman and Mighton removed all military paint, including that on the propeller and spinner, and prepared the P-39 for the Thompson Trophy Race to be held for several days over Labor Day weekend in Cleveland, Ohio, in 1946. The Airacobra now carried the civilian registration NX57591 vertically on its rudder, large Sohio decals on the aft fuselage sides, round Kendall oil decals on its doors and a large race number 12 on its forward fuselage sides.

Ortman and Mighton brought in Charles W. Bing to fly the P-39 in the race. Bing added the nickname *JUBA* diagonally to the nose behind the race number, a name based on combining his two daughters' names, Judith and Barbara. The owners' and pilot's names were added to the fuselage. *JUBA* was the third P-39 entered in the 1946 Thompson Trophy Race, with the other two Airacobras being the ill-fated *Cobra I* and the trophy winner *Cobra II*. *JUBA* was slower and was forced from the line up. Instead of the Thompson, *JUBA* raced in the Sohio Trophy Consolation Race in Cleveland on August 31, 1946 with Charles Bing at the controls. Despite showing a relatively good average speed of 276.135 miles per hour, *JUBA* finished seventh and last. NX57591 was offered for sale within the next few months.

Its next owner was Elizabeth "Betty" Haas. She was a former WASP (Women's Airforce Service Pilot) who began flying in 1941. She joined the WASPs in 1943 graduating that September. She was an active pilot with the Ferry Command flying single and multi-engine military aircraft, including B-17s and B-24s (bombers). She flew until the WASPs were disbanded in December 1944. She had never flown fighters, but had accumulated numerous flying hours in advanced trainers. While at the West Chester County Airport in White Plains, New York, near her home, she flew NX57591 on October 27, 1946. She liked the P-39 immensely and bought it on October 31, 1946, for $1,000. She remembers buying the P-39 from a Mr. A. C. Vanden-Bulcke. The P-39 was registered to Betty Haas as of December 4, 1946. She renamed her P-39 *Galloping Gertie*, a name similar to a racing P-51, *The Galloping Ghost*. Betty Haas flew *Gertie* actively for almost three and a half years. She removed the name *JUBA* and painted *Galloping Gertie* diagonally between race number 12 and the spinner. The Sohio decal was moved to the vertical fin, and a new decal from Air Carrier Maintenance was added to the aft fuselage. The P-39's spinner and propeller were painted, and the word "experimental" was stencilled on the doors. Eventually Betty Haas went to a friend of her family, world famous artist Norman Rockwell, and asked him to design a paint scheme for her P-39. The result was a beautiful red and white racing trim that complimented the long lines of the fuselage and the curves of the wing and horizontal tail. The number N57591 was carried horizontally on the rudder. The P-39 had no decals, race number nor any name while in its two-tone red and white paint scheme.

Betty Haas flew her P-39 regularly at air shows, and she competed in several races. Chuck Yeager flew it once at an air show in Philadelphia. It never placed in competition because of its generally stock condition, but it was always flown to the limit of its performance, requiring replacement of the engine at least twice with at least one emergency landing at the Jacksonville, Florida airport. Betty Haas averaged about 100 flying hours per year flying N57591. She was also a Pan American Airlines stewardess. By 1950, air racing was decreasing in the United States, operating costs for the

P-39 were rising, and Betty Haas became Mrs. Betty Haas Pfister. A family decision was made not to fly the P-39 anymore. Mrs. Pfister did not want to sell her P-39, fearing someone may be hurt flying the fighter. She decided to loan her P-39 to the National Air Museum. On January 5, 1950, she flew N57591 for her last time to Bell Aircraft Corporation in Niagara Falls, New York. Bell test pilot Joe Cannon flew N57591 for its last trip to the temporary storage hangar at O'Hare Air Force Base at Park Ridge, Illinois (which later became Chicago's O'Hare International Airport). The beautiful red and white P-39 was displayed at the O'Hare Air Force Base's open house in May 1951. The Airacobra was disassembled, pickeled and crated for storage and future restoration.

In 1956, Mrs. Pfister finally donated her P-39 to the museum. N57591 was in storage for 19 years. It was exposed to the weather during some of this period and began to deteriorate. In 1969, the P-39 was loaned to the Experimental Aircraft Association Museum in Hales Corner, Wisconsin. It was reassembled and repainted in military colors. Its military number was painted in yellow on the tail, all military stencilling was added, and Army Air Corps' insignia was placed on its fuselage and wings. Finally, *Galloping Gertie* and *B. Haas Pfister* were added to its nose and doors. On December 5, 1970, *Galloping Gertie* was fully reassembled for the first time since 1951. In 1984, the National Air and Space Museum brought 44-2433 to the suburbs southeast of Washington to its present location at the Paul E. Garber restoration facility at Silver Hill, Maryland.

As of April 1990, the National Air and Space Museum's Aeronautic Department advised that because *Gertie* was in reasonably good shape, she was not on the museum's five-year restoration schedule. If her condition deteriorates, she will be restored. When *Galloping Gertie* is restored, she will be given the color trim and markings of a P-39 from the 18th Fighter Group which flew from the Bouganville Islands, east of New Guinea. *Gertie* now sits close to a metal finish P-63, its younger sibling, waiting her turn for transfer to the museum on the Mall in the nation's capitol. She may be viewed by contacting the Garber facility and scheduling a tour.

Finland's captured P-39Q Airacobra, now in storage, but in a restorable condition. COURTESY OF THE CENTRAL FINLAND AVIATION MUSEUM

Gary Larkins' P-39Q-15-BE

Gary Larkins of Auburn, California, operates A.P., Inc. (P.O. Box 7108, Auburn, California 95608). His aircraft restoration facility has located and restored over 40 warbirds during the past 20 years, including several P-47s and P-51s. In July 1990, Mr. Larkins located a P-39 sunken in a Canadian lake, and he brought the Airacobra to California for restoration to flying condition. His Airacobra is the last known P-39 to be recovered. It holds great promise to soon become a flying restoration.

Army Air Force serial number 44-2485 is a Bell P-39Q-15-BE built under order number AC-40071, received on October 22, 1943. This P-39 was built at an unspecified cost for export to Russia. It was assembled with both a Bell data plate and a Russian export data plate, and was trimmed from the beginning in Russian markings.

44-2485 departed Buffalo on November 29, 1943, and arrived at Fort Nelson, British Columbia, in Canada by December 6, 1943. On December 6, 44-2485 was prepared for a flight to Whitehorse. Its pilot would be Lieutenant Delos R. Carpenter who was instructed to eventually fly the P-39 to Ladd Field, Alaska, where it would be turned over to a Russian ferry pilot. Lieutenant Carpenter was a pilot with the 25th Ferrying Squadron of the 7th Ferrying Group of the Air Transport Command. He had 475 hours flying Army Air Force aircraft, of which 40 were in Airacobras. He lives today in the Eldorado Hills area of California.

On December 6, Carpenter's element leader, Lieutenant Hal Coons, took off from Fort Nelson at 11:05 a.m. in another P-39 with Lieutenant Carpenter as his wingman. The two P-39s climbed through the overcast skies and headed for Whitehorse. After about an hour, they descended through the poor weather, but they became separated. Unknown to Carpenter, Coons had experienced a compass failure. The two pilots could not find one another, and Carpenter was on his own. Lieutenant Coons was eventually able to find Fort Nelson. Lieutenant Carpenter tried but could not find his leader. He dropped his belly tank when his fuel got low. He finally decided to make a wheels up landing on an unnamed and uncharted frozen lake near the Arctic Circle that had barely two inches of ice covering it. The belly landing was generally successful, and Lieutenant Carpenter did only minimal damage to his Airacobra. He buckled the right wing and tore the .50 calibre machine gun off and bent the propeller, but all else was intact. Carpenter pulled his personal equipment out. By 8:30 p.m., he was able to contact Lake Army Airways. By 3 p.m. the next day, Lieutenant Carpenter was rescued by a plane that landed on skis on the frozen lake. 44-2485 thus became one of 178 P-39s that crashed before arriving in Alaska to be delivered to the Russians.

During February 1944, the Army Air Force decided to salvage 44-2485. On February 8, one officer and 11 enlisted personnel were sent to the unnamed frozen lake. The Army team set up tents and a camp nearby. Parts were taken off the P-39 and flown out daily in the two Norseman transports as the weather allowed and delivered to Fort Smith. The Army Air Force salvaged much of the P-39, including the engine, cockpit instruments and landing gear. Other parts, such as access panels, the cowling and propeller, were removed and left on the ice near the crashlanded P-39. The weather worsened by February 27, and the two planes flew the recovery team out. One Norseman, however, crashed into a lake and exploded, killing the pilot and one crew member. When spring later followed, the ice melted on the lake, and the P-39 with its leftover parts sank as deep as 60 feet into the freshwater. Everything, however, stayed within 30 feet of the sunken Airacobra.

For many years, 44-2485's existence had been known about, but its exact location had eluded warbird finders. Gary Larkins had tried to locate the crashlanded Airacobra once before, but without success. His second trip to the Canadian wilderness in July 1990, however, would be different. The P-39 had crashed in Canada 14 miles north of the Virginia Falls on the Nahanni River, about 240 miles from Watson Lake. The Army Air Force's location coordinates from the war years were 40 miles too far north. Larkins and two divers landed on the lake in an Otter with floats. They took with them diving supplies, tools, lift bags and sonar equipment. They knew they had discovered the correct site as the remains of the U.S. Army tents and stoves were found nearby. It took two days with the sonar scanner to locate the P-39. The Airacobra's tail was found at a depth of 30 feet. This followed down to the nose at 60 feet. Much of the P-39 was encased in mud. The old fighter plane was recovered on July 19 and 20, 1990. Larkins first removed the tail section and towed it to shore attached to his rowboat. From there the horizontal stabilizer was removed. The airframe was next lifted with air bags and moved to shore where rigging cables were attached. The now tailless P-39 was then settled back onto the lake floor. Three days later, a Bell 205 helicopter arrived to pull its "ancestor" from the lake to the shore. Four and a half decades of preserving mud were removed to disclose an Airacobra remarkably free of corrosion. It then took the helicopter over nine hours to fly the Airacobra to Watson Lake while reaching altitudes as high as 14,000 feet to get the P-39 over the mountains. The wings were removed at Watson Lake, and 44-2485 was prepared for a trip by trailer to California for a complete restoration.

Today, 44-2485 is in the early stages of being restored to airworthy status. It has an excellent airframe. Gary Larkins has two other parts P-39s for usage in rebuilding this latest Airacobra. He plans to build a second, static-only Airacobra from the remaining parts. He has a zero-time Allison engine for 44-2485 as well as many other P-39 parts still in their factory boxes, such as windshield and side glass components. 44-2485 is estimated to take two years to restore. It will be repainted in Russian markings for display and flown ocassionally. Mr. Larkins hopes eventually to fly his restored P-39 with a P-40 and B-25 also trimmed in Russian markings to recreate the route once flown to Russia by so many different Lend-Lease aircraft during World War II.

Recovering 44-2485 from sixty feet of water and transporting it away from the Canadian wilderness is a monumental task as these pictures confirm.
COURTESY GARY LARKINS

Finland's P-39Q-15-BE

Other publications reported an ex-British export Airacobra I transferred to the Russians exists in Finland at the Finnair Aviation College after being captured. A second P-39, a P-39Q, Army Air Force serial number 44-2664, has been reported as a part of the Finnish National Collection. Letters to the Finnair Aviation College (the Finnish Aviation Museum, Ilmailumuseo, Tietotie 3, SF-01530, Vantaa, Finland) and the Central Finland Aviation Museum (Keski-Suomen Ilmailumuseo, Kuikantie 1, SF-41160, Tikkakoski, Finland), have confirmed the Airacobra I does not exist. The Central Finland Aviation Museum does have one unrestored P-39Q in its collection. It is a composite aircraft consisting of a fuselage from a Russian P-39Q-15-BE, Army Air Force serial number 44-2664, which made a forced landing in Aunus in June 1944, and wings from a P-39Q-20-BE, Army Air Force serial number 44-3255, which made a forced landing at Inkeroinen on June 17, 1944. The fuselage still bears its Russian markings and the number 26 on its nose.

44-2664 was delivered on November 5,1943, under contract AC-40071. It was available for delivery to the Russians on December 1, 1943. It arrived at Fairbanks, Alaska, on December 30, 1943, and transferred to the Russians on January 12, 1944. It most likely served in Russia with 191 AP, a fighter squadron based at Leningrad. It is painted olive drab with neutral grey undersides. According to the museum, "44-2664 was one of two P-39Qs which made a forced landing on a marsh after losing their bearings and running out of fuel. The aircraft were only slightly damaged and the pilots tried to get back to their own side. Near Hamina, however, they were caught, and they did not surrender. In the ensuing skirmish, one of them was killed and the other wounded."

The P-39 was kept at the Finnish Air Force depot at Tampere until 1981 when it came under the Ilmailumuseo's control after nearly forty years of storage in damp areas. All instruments and electrical equipment were removed. "The fin and rudder were accidentally changed to those of a Yak-9!" according to the museum. The engine was checked and lubricated. This Airacobra is unrestored and in need of numerous parts. It will be returned to static display condition.

The Air Force Museum's P-39Q-20-BE

The Air Force Museum at Wright-Patterson Air Force Base in Dayton, Ohio, has a P-39Q-20-BE, Army Air Force serial 44-3887. This P-39 was built under contract AC-40071. It was accepted by the Army Air Force on February 13, 1944, and delivered on February 21, 1944, but to an unknown Army base location. It was available on March 8, 1944. It was sent to an unnamed air base in Minneapolis on September 22, 1944. It was then referred to as an RP-39Q. It was ferried to Cincinnati on October 6, 1944, then returned to Minneapolis on January 16, 1945, and again to Cincinnati on May 5, 1945, when it was still referred to as an RP-39Q. Sometime during its military career, this Airacobra was reconfigured to a two-seater TP-39Q. It never left the United States. When it was stricken from the inventory is not known. It was probably sold by the War Assets Administration by 1946. The TP-39Q's first civilian owner is unknown but most likely lived in Illinois.

The Airacobra's second civilian owner was Jack B. Hardwick. During the Second World War, Hardwick was a Ferry Command pilot. During 1942, he made several hundred flights from the Bell plant in Niagara Falls, New York, to Anchorage, Alaska, ferrying new P-39s to the Russians under America's Lend-Lease program. After the war, Hardwick established the Hardwick Aircraft Company in El Monte (northern Los Angeles), California. He soon became a world traveler, aircraft exporter and motion picture stunt pilot. While flying a P-38 Lightning to an air show in 1947, Hardwick made an emergency landing at an air field in central Illinois. He discovered this TP-39Q there. The first owner was afraid of the Airacobra, and Hardwick was able to buy the TP-39Q for $250. He test flew it, but later trucked it to California. The TP-39Q was not in very good shape when located. It deteriorated to a near derelict while sitting in Hardwick's aircraft yard. The TP-39Q was rediscovered by the 1960s in poor condition among the remains of other aircraft. Hardwick restored it using parts from other P-39s as far away as northern Alaska. He reconfigured the Airacobra to a single-seat P-39Q by removing the TP-39 conversion kit. Hardwick Aircraft Company, incidentally, does not exist today.

In July 1966, the freshly restored P-39Q was flown to the Air Force Museum. The Air Force Museum's Airacobra today is painted not as P-39Q but rather as a P-39J flown by Lieutenant Leslie Spoontz (now a retired United States Air Force Colonel) of the 57th Fighter Squadron based at Kodiak and Adak Islands during the Aleutian (Alaska) Campaign in 1942. It still retains its P-39Q tail number of 43887 whereas Spoontz's P-39, which is believed to have been a P-39F and not a P-39J, had the tail number of 17341.

The Air Force Museum's P-39Q-20-BE on display at Wright-Patterson Air Force Base in Dayton, Ohio. COURTESY AIR FORCE MUSEUM

The "newest" Airacobra belongs to the Kalamazoo Aviation History Museum. It is today the only other flyable P-39 beside the one operated by the Confederate Air Force. COURTESY KALAMAZOO AVIATION HISTORY MUSEUM

The Kalamazoo Air Zoo's RP-39Q-20-BE

The Kalamazoo Aviation History Museum (3101 East Milham Road, Kalamazoo, Michigan 49002) is the proud home of the other flying P-39 in the world today. This P-39 is also the "newest" Airacobra in existence. United States Army Air Force serial number 44-3908 is a Bell RP-39Q-20-BE Airacobra. Bell built it without any armament under contract AC-40071 at an unconfirmed cost. It was powered by an Allison V-1710-85-E19 engine developing 1,125 horsepower. It was delivered to the Army Air Force on February 12, 1944. It was assigned to the Victorville, California, Training Command with the 3035th Base Unit on September 16, 1944. It was transferred to the Naples, Florida, Training Command with the 2119th Base Unit Fighter Group, 79th Experimental Flight Test Center on December 10, 1944. On July 14, 1945, it was transferred to the Buckingham, Florida, Training Command with the 2117th Base Unit Fighter Group, 79th Experimental Flight Test Center. On October 18, 1945, it was transferred to the Tyndall, Florida, Training Command with the 2135th Base Unit Training. On November 9, 1945, it was turned over to the Reconstruction Finance Corporation at Altus Field, Oklahoma. In April 1946, the War Assets Administration sold 44-3908 to Mr. W. H. Ostenberg of Scotts Bluff, Nebraska, who obtained the civilian registration NX4829N for the Airacobra. The first civilian paint scheme was medium green with the registration number painted vertically on the tail. The second paint scheme was yellow with race number 15 on the fuselage. The third was white and blue with red trim.

The second owner was Paul Addy of Fostoria, Ohio in 1950. From 1957 to 1963, NX4829N was owned by E. D. Weiner of Hayward, California. The P-39 was next owned by Robert M. Lindquist of Santa Ana, California, from 1963 to 1966, then Donald D. Randall of the same city until 1969. In August 1972, Mira Slovak purchased the Airacobra while dismantled in storage at the Orange County Airport in California. It was moved to Van Nuys where Dick Martin and his staff restored it. Its civilian registration was changed to N40A. Mr. Slovak obtained sponsorship from the Mennen Corporation and modified the P-39 for air racing. He added a new Allison V-1710-143 engine developing up to 2,000 horsepower from a P-82 Twin Mustang. He briefly used a four-bladed propeller and added dorsal and ventral fuselage fins for extra stability, but the different propeller proved too unstable. He then returned to a three-bladed unit. A P-63 windshield and Bearcat wheels and brakes were installed. N40A was repainted glossy white overall with green and gold trim. Finally "Mr. Mennen" was added to the nose cowling and across the underside of the wing. It was then raced with number 21 on its rudder.

Mr. Slovak flew N40A to Reno, Nevada, on September 13, 1972, for the Unlimited Class pylon air races but arrived too late because of mechanical problems. The Airacobra was not allowed to compete and instead flew twice in exhibition. N40A was generally not competitive for air racing. It was retired as a result. It returned to California but was flown infrequently, and Mennen soon stopped its sponsorship. Mira Slovak advertised the P-39 for sale. He expressed interest in selling to the Confederate Air Force. By 1975, Ed Messick and Larry Irvine of the Confederate Air Force entered into active negotiation to buy N40A. The initial asking price was $100,000. After months of discussion, Messick and Irvine bought N40A in July 1975 for $70,000, but no spare P-39 parts were added to the deal. On July 29, 1975, Mira Slovak flew the P-39 from Mojave, California, to San Antonio, Texas. The flight took five hours. Slovak flew the P-39 to Messick and Irvine's Rebel Aviation. The Airacobra was still painted white and green.

Messick and Irvine did a complete overhaul and airframe check of N40A. The additional fuselage fins were removed. The Allison V-1710-143 engine was examined and found in good condition. A transponder, navcom and an avionics sub-panel were added in the cockpit. A second starting battery was fitted in the nose along with a 28-gallon water tank and spray bar to cool the engine while taxiing. Better access to the oxygen system was completed. The Airacobra had no real guns, but a simulated cannon was added to the propeller hub. Finally, the Airacobra was repainted in a military scheme, but this time as a P-400 export Airacobra, which is British three-color camouflage. P-39Qs, such as this actual aircraft, never historically used this paint scheme. N40A represents an earlier Bell Model 14 export Airacobra of 1941 vintage, an Airacobra given back to the United States by the British and later flown by the Army Air Corps in the Pacific Theatre against the Japanese forces. N40A flew in the late 1970s with the Confederate Air Force along with the only other flying P-39 in the world discussed earlier. On October 23, 1981, N40A was acquired by Pete and Sue Parrish of Kalamazoo, Michigan. They placed N40A in their private collection at the Kalamazoo Air Museum where it resides today, still trimmed in its beautiful P-400 colors. Although this P-39Q has not flown for a few years, "it is maintained in flying condition with all systems ready to go," according to the museum's executive director, Robert E. Ellis.

These two pages contain four original Bell Aircraft Corp. factory sketches of its new Model 4, from the 1936-37 era. BELL AIRCRAFT CORP. VIA TRUMAN A. PARTRIDGE, SR.

BELL AIRCRAFT CORP.
BUFFALO, N. Y.

BELL AIRCRAFT CORP.
BUFFALO, N. Y.

BIBLIOGRAPHY

The author wishes to acknowledge with thanks the following source books, magazines and articles used to research this book.

BOOKS

Angelucci, Enzo. *The American Fighter.* New York, NY: Orion Books, 1985.

Chapman, John and Goodall, Geoff. *Warbirds Worldwide Directory.* Leicester, England: Midland Counties Publications, 1989.

Cloe, John H. *Top Cover for America, The Air Force in Alaska 1920-1983.* Missoula, MT: Pictorial Histories Publishing Co., 1984.

Craven, Wesley F. and Cate, James L. *The Army Air Forces in World War II, Volumes One through Seven.* Chicago, IL: The University of Chicago Press, 1948.

Davis, Larry. *Air War Over Korea.* Carrollton, TX: Squadron/Signal Publications, Inc., 1982.

Ethell, Jeffrey. *The Great Book of World War II Airplanes.* Tokyo, Japan: Wing and Anchor Press; and New York, NY: Bonanza Books, 1984.

Francillon, Dr. Rene J. *American Fighters of World War Two, Volume One.* Chalfont St. Giles, Bucks, England: Hylton Lacy, 1968.

Green, William. *War Planes of the Second World War, Fighters, Volume Four.* Garden City, NY: Hanover House, 1961.

Huntington, Roger. *Thompson Trophy Racers.* Osceola, WI: Motorbooks International, 1989.

Jablonski, Edward. *Airwar.* Garden City, NY: Doubleday and Company, 1971.

McDowell, Ernie. *P-39 Airacobra in Action.* Carrollton, TX: Squadron/Signal Publications, 1980.

Norton, Donald J. *Larry, A Biography of Lawrence D. Bell.* Chicago, IL: Nelson-Hall Inc., 1981.

Ogden, Robert. *The Aircraft Museums and Collections of North America.* Middlesex, England: The Aviation Hobby Shop, 1988.

Robinson, Anthony. *The Encyclopedia of American Aircraft.* New York, NY: A&W Publishers, 1979.

Siefring, Thomas A. *U.S. Air Force in World War II.* Secaucus, NJ: Chartwell Books, Inc., 1977.

Yeager, Chuck. *Yeager: An Autobiography.* New York, NY: Bantam Books, Inc., 1985.

Zemke, Hub. *Zemke's Wolf Pack.* New York, NY: Orion Books, 1989.

________. *Jane's Fighting Aircraft of World War II.* New York, NY: Military Press, 1946/47, republished 1989.

ARTICLES

Beck, Norman. "From the Ashes," *Air Classics,* December 1983, pp. 14-18.

Bell, Lawrence D. "Statement Before The Sub-Committee on Aircraft and Light Metals of the Special Committee Investigating the National Defense Program, United States Senate," October 10, 1945.

Clayton, Mark. "Australian Airacobras," *FlyPast*, Issue No. 39, October 1984, pp. 14-15.

Essex, Allen. "Bell P-39 Airacobra, An Anniversary Tale," *CAF Dispatch*, May/June 1989, pp. 10-11.

Fornoff, Art. *News from the Home Front to the Bell Service Representative,* various issues referred to between March 18, 1943 and August 5, 1943.

Furler, E. H., Jr. "Cobras for the Navy," *Air Classics*, January 1984, pp. 14 to 20.

Furler, E. H., Jr. "From Kangaroos to Bananas," *Air Classics*, June 1984, pp. 20 to 29.

Furler, E. H., Jr. "The Combat Story of the Bell P-400 Airacobra," *Air Classics*, October 1983, pp. 20 to 27, 70, 80 and 81.

Gorshenin, Vladimir. "A Gap in Glasnost," *Air Force Magazine*, April 1990, pp. 98-101.

Height, Andy and Coggan, Paul A. "Filming Memphis Belle-Part One, The Bombers," *Warbirds Worldwide*, Number 10, Volume Three, Number Two, pp. 23.

Hoy, Bruce. "Preservation Project." *FlyPast*, Number 64, November 1986, pp. 58.

Johnsen, Fred. "Small Fry," *Warbirds International,* July/August 1990, pp. 46-47.

Klepper, Dennis. "The XFL-1 Airabonita—First and Last," *Tester*, October 11, 1974, pp. (unknown).

Matthews, Birch J. "Airacobra in Retrospect," *A Half Century of Fighter Aircraft Development—2nd Annual Aerospace Historical Symposium* (Printed Courtesy of TRW Systems Group, TRW Inc.), March 23, 1976, pp. 1-27.

Miller, E. Eugene. "Design Analysis of the Bell Airacobra," *Aviation*, May 1943, pp. 126-156.

Neill, Randy M. "Profile of a CAF Project Officer: Virgil E. Sansing," *CAF Dispatch*, May/June 1989, pp. 16.

Niessen, __________. "The Last Airacobras," *Air Classics*, September 1977, pp. 32-41, 97-98.

O'Leary, Michael. "Cobra With A Cannon!," *Warbirds International*, Sep./Oct. 1988, pp. 14-31, 72-88.

Ott, Betty J. "P-39 Plucked from Jungle 'Lands' in Naval Park," *Buffalo Courier-Express*, March 29, 1981, pp. F-5.

Partridge, Sr., Truman A. "Snooks 2nd," *Air Classics*, June 1982, pp. 42-45, 81-82.

Partridge, Sr. Truman A. "Snooks 2nd . . . A P-39 Comes Home," *Warbirds*, September 14, 1984, pp. 12-14.

Trimble, Robert L. "Bell's Iron Dog," Part One. *Air Classics*, December 1982, pp. 28-31, 64-76; Part Two, *Air Classics*, January 1983, pp. 19 to 26, 76 to 80; Part Three, *Air Classics*, March 1983, pp. 22 to 33, 44 to 47.

Veronico, Nick. "Airacobra Recovered From Canadian Lake," *IN FLIGHT Aviation News Monthly*, September 1990, pp. 25-26.

Woodson, O. L. "How Airacobras Are Built," *American Machinist*, November 12, 1941, pp. 1-16.

__________. *The Bellringer*, December, 1940 to November-December, 1945, various articles quoted and paraphrased as applicable.

__________. *Bell Serviceman*, January 1, 1943, and subsequent issues, various articles quoted and paraphrased as applicable.

__________. "Airabonita," *Naval Aviation News*, December 1980, pp. 24-25.

__________. "Bell P-39 Airacobra History," Speech given by the Confederate Air Force at the 50th Anniversary on April 8, 1989 in San Marcos, Texas, pp. 1-3.

__________. "Cobra," *Modelcraft*, International Plastic Modellers Society of Australia, Numbers 1 and 2, 1974.

__________. "More Background on the Museum's P-39Q," *Warbirds of America News*, January 1971, pp. 18.

__________. "YAF's Last Stand," *FlyPast*, Number 40, November 1984, pp. 22-23.

Lend-Lease P-39s at Great Falls, Mont., lined up for delivery to the Russians in Alaska. STAN COHEN COLLECTION

ABOUT THE AUTHOR

Rick Mitchell is a graduate of the University of Maryland at College Park with a degree in Business. By profession, he is a Claim Technical Representative with Aetna Life and Casualty Company where he recently completed 15 years service.

In 1983, after restoring a 1966 Ford Mustang, Rick began writing about early Mustangs. He published his own typeset newsletters for several years, *Sprint Print* and later *Six Classics*. These feature newsletters were dedicated to the six-cylinder-powered early Mustangs. Many of his articles were republished in *Mustang Times,* the monthly magazine of the Mustang Club of America. Later, Rick was asked to be their contributing editor, a position he served in for two years while continuing to write his own publications. Rick also had several feature articles published in *Mustang Monthly Magazine.*

In 1988, Rick decided to write his first book, but on a different topic. He has an avid interest in aviation, especially fighter planes from World War II to the present. He is also the son of a World War II fighter pilot who continued to fly fighters until 1975 while with the Maryland Air National Guard. His father was the Group Commander until 1976. In December 1988, Rick volunteered to research and compile the *History of the Maryland Air National Guard*, a unit first established in 1921. The book that resulted was published by the government in December 1989. It is currently in its second printing with over 4,000 copies. His *Airacobra Advantage: The Flying Cannon* is Rick's first privately developed book. Rick has used many of the skills developed in his career as an accident investigator to review the history of the P-39 from several perspectives while providing one-on-one interviews discussing the Airacobra to breathe additional life into the text, a technique used by insurance company representatives.

Rick is a lifelong resident of suburban Baltimore where he lives with his wife, Dorothy, nine-year-old son, Steven, and two-year-old daughter, Kelly. He is currently researching and developing a new project on the North American Aviation F-86 Sabre Jet.

POSTSCRIPT

As this book goes to press in early 1992, the author is pleased to announce that N.M. Armstrong's P-39Q, serial number 42-19993, is now proudly owned by the Santa Monica Museum of Flying, located at the Santa Monica Airport, 2772 Donald Douglas Loop North, Santa Monica, California 90405. 42-19993's history through 1989 was described earlier. At some time between then and 1991, 42-19993 was transferred from Australia to the United States by Don Whittington. Because the author was never able to confirm the tail number on Mr. Whittington's Airacobra also discussed earlier, it is not known whether 42-19993 was Mr. Whittington's Airacobra as reviewed earlier in this text or a different P-39.

It is known that during 1991, 42-19993 was purchased by the Museum of Flying for restoration to *flying* status. The author was able to update 42-19993's history with Bruce Lockwood, the Museum of Flying's restoration director, in late December 1991 to confirm 42-19993's restoration to flying status will begin by spring 1992. The corrosion in this Airacobra has been described as minimal, and the wing's restoration will not be overly difficult. 42-19993 will take approximately two years to rebuild while in the company of two other World War Two fighters under repair, a Bearcat and a recently acquired Mitsubishi A6M3 Zero. Watch for 42-19993 to take to the skies once again flying formation with a restored Zero!